CELEBRATING *the* ~ BEAN ~

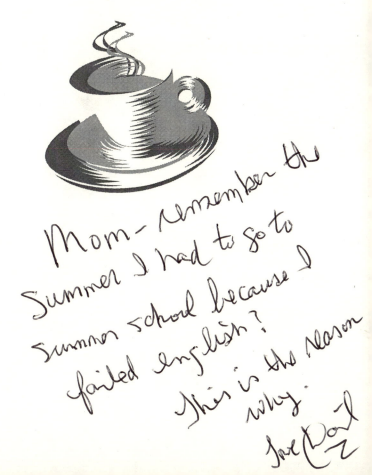

Mom — Remember the summer I had to go to summer school because I failed English? This is the reason why.

Love Paul

CELEBRATING the BEAN

The Ultimate Coffee Lover's Book
☞ For Ultimate Coffee Lovers ☜

DAVID STOCKDALE

TATE PUBLISHING & *Enterprises*

TATE PUBLISHING
& *Enterprises*

Tate Publishing is committed to excellence in the publishing industry. Our staff of highly trained professionals, including editors, graphic designers, and marketing personnel, work together to produce the very finest books available. The company reflects the philosophy established by the founders, based on Psalms 68:11,

"THE LORD GAVE THE WORD AND GREAT WAS THE COMPANY OF THOSE WHO PUBLISHED IT."

If you would like further information, please contact us:
1.888.361.9473 | www.tatepublishing.com
TATE PUBLISHING & *Enterprises*, LLC | 127 E. Trade Center Terrace
Mustang, Oklahoma 73064 USA

Celebrating the Bean
Copyright © 2007 by David Stockdale. All rights reserved.

No part of this publication may be reproduced, stored in a retrieval system or transmitted in any way by any means, electronic, mechanical, photocopy, recording or otherwise without the prior permission of the author except as provided by USA copyright law.

Book design copyright © 2007 by Tate Publishing, LLC. All rights reserved.
Cover design Leah Leflore
Interior design Janae Glass
Published in the United States of America

ISBN: 1-6024701-0-3

06.12.

Acknowledgements

The following is a very special Thank You to the people who accompanied me on my journey.

To Lorraine Martineau, a colleague and aspiring professional photographer, for taking your time and effort to bring the photographs in my book to life.

To Tim Schoonmaker, for your phenomenal patience and professionalism. You were always flexible with time management. When I needed the time to write or do anything at all related to my book you were there.

To Michele Lerow and Yvonne Stillpass, the marketing team at Lakewood Ranch Medical Center, for your input and assistance in putting me in touch with the people that you thought could help my cause.

To Barbara, you and I both understand the meaning of being in the right place at the right time.

And finally, to my family and friends, all of whom fully understand through dealing with me the highs and the lows of the whole creative process.

Thank You.

Table of contents

1) Forward: The power of the spoken word   9
2) Did you know? Interesting factoids about the celebrated bean.   13
3) Early Beginnings: A whimsical trek through the history of coffee.   15
4) The Basics of Brewing: Baby your beans...   21
5) The Brewers: discover the amazing versatility of the celebrated coffee bean.   27
6) Espresso Yourself! Step by step instructions- absolutely everything you need to know to produce the perfect espresso, cappuccino, café latte, and café mocha at home.   39
7) Coffee Recipes: Some submitted by fellow coffee lovers, just like you.   53
    a) Submitted recipes
    b) Hot regular brewed coffee drinks
    c) Cold regular brewed coffee drinks
    d) Hot espresso based coffee drinks
    e) Cold espresso based coffee drinks
    f) Utilizing coffee in entrees
    g) Utilizing coffee in desserts
8) Did you know? A few more interesting coffee factoids.   169

Foreword

I have always been a coffee fan. It is my passion. For reasons unknown I sat down one day and put pen to paper. Ink to parchment. My thoughts and feelings flowed. Deep inside I knew I had to share my passion of coffee with others. Finishing my original manuscript, I looked for somebody to take my primitive lines from ink to the printed page. After going down numerous avenues to no avail, I reached a dead end. One day, on my way to work in a local hospital, I made a plea to God. I spoke these words aloud. My plea was as simple as this. "God...I need somebody to type my manuscript. I believe that you will send somebody to me today." Words, spoken aloud, in the privacy of my own car. That day at lunch, I sat alone at a table, reviewing my book. A woman, who volunteers her time at the hospital, by the name of Barbara Patterson, stopped by my table. She said, and I quote, "What are you looking at?" I explained I had gathered some information about my passion, coffee, and had written it down. Her next words absolutely floored me. She said "I used to teach typing in high school. I just moved into a new condominium and have extra time on my hands. Can I help you with that?" I would never allow anybody to take my manuscript. I had put many hours into it and it was dear to me. However, that surreal meeting with Barbara, my miracle, let me let loose of the written pages...and she walked away that day with my book. You are reading the result of that moment...my miracle.

Timeline: July, 1969   Location: Outer Space.

The surface of the moon. Four hours before the first moonwalk, Houston Control received this message: "Excuse me for a minute. I am going to have a cup of coffee!"

Coffee... The name alone conjures up images, thoughts, and impressions.

A quick brew in the morning on your way to work. Long, slow afternoons on the verandah, savoring a rich bowlful. An after-dinner indulgence, enjoyed over your favorite dessert. Coffee has found its way into the lives of millions of people.

It is the ultimate aromatic. Envision being warm and snuggly under the blankets. Something is tugging at your senses. Well, one of your senses.

Even though you are three doors down, you can't escape the delightful smell wafting from your kitchen. It's intoxicating. It will make you get out of bed and head to the hub of your home. This is not to say that you will indulge in a freshly brewed cup. Coffee, as aromatic as it is, is an acquired taste. Some would argue that it is too acidic, or too strong. Many of these doubters, however, have succumbed to the passion of drinking coffee by 'mellowing out' their brew with cream and sugar. Any way you drink it, whether black, light, hot, cold, sweetened, or unsweetened, it's definitely a pleasure. We as human beings are sociable creatures. What better way to socialize than over a perfect cup of coffee? Although specialty coffee drinks are growing in leaps and bounds, they are definitely not *'new.'*

Coffee has been around a long time. As legend would

have it, sometime between 600-800 A.D., a young goat herder by the name of Kaldi, who resided in Ethiopia, was tending his goats. He observed them eating the red berries of a nearby bush. Shortly thereafter, the goats began to frolic and play merrily. Kaldi, inquisitive goat herder that he was, decided to investigate.

He found that, after eating the ripe red berries, he, too, experienced the same stimulating effect. Neighboring monks soon heard about this remarkable berry. They would dry the berries so they could transport them to far off monasteries. When they arrived at a monastery, they would soak the dried berries in water. They would then eat the berry and drink the caffeine ingested water. In doing this, they believed their senses were more acute during prayer. Soon after, the early Africans started to mix coffee with fat to carry with them when they needed to refuel on their journeys. These were meager beginnings, but the birth of coffee had begun!

Did you know?

- Coffee is actually a fruit! When the ripe red cherries of the coffee plant obtain a brilliant red hue, they are hand-picked, leaving the green cherries behind. As the green cherries ripen, the plant will be revisited every eight to ten days until it is harvested completely.

- Some coffee producing countries schedule the school year around the harvest time so that the children can assist in picking the ripe, red cherries. The act of picking only the red cherries is very labor intensive, but it is imperative in producing the best Arabica coffee.

- There are two types of coffee beans: Arabica (the very best and hand picked) grown at elevations of 2000 feet and above, and Robusta, a heartier plant grown at lower altitudes.

- Inside the cherry are two green coffee beans which sit side by side. Sometimes only one round bean is produced. This is called a peaberry. Some people dispute that the peaberry is a superior bean, due to all of the essence of the coffee being put into one bean, and not into two.

- Robusta beans contain twice the caffeine as Arabica beans.

- The ripe red cherries are husked, the green coffee beans dried, then graded according to size. Millions of bags of green coffee beans are exported from producing countries every year.

- The United States alone imports over 2.5 million pounds of green coffee beans per year, roughly ⅓ of all coffee exported.

- It takes a coffee plant four years to reach maturity. Each plant produces only one pound of coffee per year and, if cared for, can be harvested 20 years or more.

- There are roughly 2000 cherries (or 4000 roasted coffee beans in each pound of coffee.

- Dollar wise, coffee is second only to oil on the world's commodity market.

- Now, put *that* in your coffee maker and brew it . . .

-Interesting-!

Early Beginnings . . .

Circa 600-850 A.D.
An Ethiopian goat herder named Kaldi is credited by some for *discovering* coffee. The early Africans combine coffee with fat, realizing the stimulating result of eating the mixture gives them more energy.

1100's
The first coffee plants are cultivated by the Arabs. They find that by roasting the beans and boiling them in water they create a brew that is not only stimulating, but enjoyable. Coffee becomes so popular in their culture that it is thrown at the feet of the bride at Arabic weddings as a religious offering. It becomes a staple in Arabic homes, and failing to keep a supply for one's wife was considered *grounds for divorce*. The early Arabs called their brew quahwa, which means *that which prevents sleep*.

1200's - 1300's
The use of coffee increases dramatically. Through trade, it crosses borders, finding its way as far as Turkey and Spain.

1400's
The world's first coffee house, KIVA HAN, is opened in Turkey.

1500's
In Saudi Arabian Mecca, Governor Khair Beg tries to ban coffee. Not a coffee fan, he is afraid his subject's love of coffee will overthrow his rule. The Sultan believes that coffee is sacred and has Governor Beg executed.

1600's
In Rome the priests are up in arms. They perceive the stimulating brew a thing of evil which alters the mind. They appeal to Pope Clement VIII to ban this 'devil's drink.' However, Pope Clement, as it turns out, is a coffee fan and baptizes it as a Christian drink.

Coffee is seen in Europe as a medical remedy and is soon being sold in local pharmacies.

Coffee houses are being opened all over Europe, with many local businessmen patronizing. It is said that coffee sharpens the mind for clarity.

It is believed that milk was first added to coffee in Holland, in order to reduce acidity.

1700's
In Paris, King Louis XIV is presented with a coffee plant. It is said that sugar was first added to coffee in his court.

In Boston, the colonists protest the increased tax on tea by the English Government. They dump tons of tea from an English cargo ship into Boston Harbor. Coffee becomes a staple in American homes and a symbol of patriotism.

In New York City, merchants meet at Tontine Coffee House. They exchange ideas and grow their businesses by trading goods and monies. Meager origins, but the Tontine Coffee House grew into the now famous New York Stock Exchange.

1800's
In London, the coffee houses were busy. As in earlier New York, many business deals were being conducted. A stimulating cup of coffee sharpened the mind. In order to have their cup delivered more quickly, patrons designed a box, labeled 'to ensure promptness.' They would put a pence in the box for the server, so as to obtain their brew more quickly. 'To ensure promptness,' shortened to *'tep'*, is credited as the origin of *'tipping.'*

Lloyds of London, who insure some of the world's costliest goods, was originally a coffee house.

Coffee brewing equipment and coffee bean roasters are at their earliest concepts. The first espresso coffee maker is invented in France. It is discovered that hot air is a good method to roast the green coffee beans to the desired brown hue.

1900's

The first drip coffee maker is invented by Melitta Bentz, a German housewife. She uses a filter made of blotting paper taken from her oldest son's notebook.

Decaffeinated coffee is invented in America, named 'Sanka,' from the French words sans caffeine (without caffeine).

Instant coffee is invented by a Japanese-American chemist, Satori Kato.

After World War I, English soldiers return home. Having little tea but ample coffee rations at war, they start a revival of coffee in England.

After World War II, employers realize employees work longer and harder after drinking coffee--this was probably the origin of the now famous *coffee break.*

2000's

Coffee is the world's most consumed beverage, with more than 400 billion cups being enjoyed every year.

Coffee sales are still growing in leaps and bounds. New coffee houses are emerging every day. Even gas stations now sell gourmet Arabica coffees by the cup.

In a culture that thoroughly embraces the celebrated coffee bean, I have decided to give you a comprehensive guide to brewing the perfect cup, and some absolutely awesome recipes you can try at home. I have included recipes submitted to me from people just like you, true coffee lovers. Pour yourself a cup and come explore with me the versatile coffee bean.

The basics of brewing

There are three key ingredients to making the best cup of coffee at home. The number one ingredient, in my opinion, is the water. Depending on where you live, the quality of water coming out of your taps can vary greatly. Consider this - 98% of a cup of coffee is water. Taking that fact in hand, you can understand its significance. Whether you have a home-installed water filtration system, or a manual pour-over filter, utilize it every time you make your favorite brew. You will notice the difference!

Number two on the list? Quality coffee. I suggest buying only whole bean Arabica coffee and grinding it yourself. Coffee begins to deteriorate at the very moment it is ground, due to its contact with air. Keep whole bean coffee in an airtight glass container in a cool, dry, dark place. A glass container will not absorb the natural oil contained in coffee. If coffee is kept too long in a container such as plastic, the container will absorb the stale oil and infect the fresh coffee beans added to it. Although the coffee will keep up to 30 days, I suggest that you buy only enough for a two week period. This will assure the optimum freshness. As important as the coffee you purchase, an appropriate coffee grinder is required. There are two types of grinders you can utilize for every day brewing: the blade grinder and the burr grinder. I will explain the pros and cons of each grinder in the EspressoYourself chapter of the book.

Finally , the third key ingredient--the coffee brewer. There are many variations available on the market from which to choose. Each is unique in design. Some will require a finer grind of coffee, some a coarser grind. Some will produce a heavier brew, some a lighter brew. As we explore different brewers and brewing techniques, you will be amazed at how versatile the celebrated bean is.

I simply ask you to remember this. A cup of coffee is only as good as the equipment used to produce it. The number one thing to remember about maintaining your brewer is to keep it clean. Coffee beans contain natural oils. It is these oils that heat and expand during roasting, creating the heady aroma and light or dark hue of the roasted coffee bean. However, these oils can adhere to your brewer and, if not cleaned, can build up over time. The residual oil will become rancid, resulting in a bitter brew. So keep it clean.

We have covered all of the basic bases, now it's time to explore all the different ways to brew our favorite pleasure. The first step is to take your whole bean coffee and grind it. Each brewer requires its own grind and you can achieve this with the proper grinder. The two most popular types of grinders available are the blade grinder and the burr grinder.

The blade type is the most common grinder. It contains a well with a sharp blade in the bottom. Begin by measuring your whole bean coffee into the well. If you are using the coffee brewer found in most homes, the electric drip, measure two tablespoons of coffee per six ounce cup. This is only a rule of thumb, you will find your measurements according to your personal taste.

Put the lid on your grinder and press the button. The blade 'chops' the coffee beans--the longer you keep the button down, the finer the coffee will be. You will find that timing your length of grind will result in a consistent brew. My blade grinder takes 13-15 seconds to achieve the best extraction. Experiment and you will soon find what works best for you.

Invest in a grinder brush!

The burr grinder is the second most used in residential homes. It is used in coffee houses to grind their espresso for specialty drinks such as cappuccinos and lattes. The difference is in its design. It contains a coffee bean chamber which is placed directly above two burr blades. The blades are circular and sit side by side. When the chamber is opened, the coffee beans fall between the rotating blades. The blades can be turned closer together to obtain a fine grind, or farther apart for a coarser grind. For optimum quality and consistency at home, the burr grinder is the way to go.

Remember to keep the coffee bean chamber free of oil!

The brewers

Another day, another cup of coffee . . . .

Easily the most popular, and undoubtedly used in almost every home, is the electric drip machine. They got their big push into civilian homes in the 1950's when restaurant owners popularized them. The early machines were big and clunky; however, they did their job. They filled the restaurant with a comforting aroma that awakened many a sleepy eyed early morning diner.

Today's modern versions are produced with many options: automatic timers, digital clocks, automatic shut off, permanent gold filters, to name a few.

You can choose from many name brands. Whatever electric drip brewer you choose, to get the optimum performance for the perfect cup, follow these drip tips:

- Use cold, fresh, filtered water. Fresh water contains more oxygen, which enhances flavor.
- Use the correct amount of freshly ground coffee.
- Buy a machine with a cone-shaped filter. Due to its shape, it ensures better extraction. When the heated water enters the cone, it is taken from a wide surface to a point, concentrating it.

A flat-bottomed filter does not utilize this, thus valu

able flavor is lost. You will also use more coffee grounds to get the flavor you want.
- Always brew at least ¾ of your brewer's cup capacity. Every drip coffee maker contains a heating element. The heating element takes some time to reach the optimum temperature. Brewing half a pot does not allow the element to do its job, resulting in a warmer and weaker brew.
- Transfer your freshly brewed coffee into a preheated insulated carafe or thermos.
If left on the heat, it will scorch, resulting in a bitter cup.

For quality brewers, visit Capresso.com.

Enjoy!

TIP: To maintain ultimate performance from your electric drip machine, the water lines need to be cleaned periodically. The lines take the water from the reservoir, through the heating element, and finally into the brew basket. Clean lines ensure the optimum heated water temperature required for the perfect cup. When heated water is passed through the line, calcium can build up inhibiting the transfer of heat from the heating element. It also will restrict the flow of the water into the ground coffee.

There are commercial cleaners available which will dissolve the calcium, or you can use regular white distilled vinegar. First make sure your brewer is unplugged. Begin by filling the water reservoir with your choice of cleaner. If using white distilled vinegar, put in three cups. If you are using a commercial cleaner, follow package instructions. Take the brew basket off and place the coffee pot on the warmer. Plug in the coffee maker and turn it on. When the liquid begins to flow through the brew head, turn the coffee maker off. This ensures that the cleaner remains in the lines. After ten minutes, turn the machine on and let more of a cleaner flow into the carafe. Turn off again. Two 10 minute intervals will assure that the cleaner has dissolved any impurities in the lines. Now run at least three full pots of water through your machine to ensure you don't get any residual cleaner in your brew. Finally, wipe the brew head to remove any oils that may remain. It is a good idea to wipe the brew head regularly after brewing coffee . . .

Before the electric drip machine was popular, people would boil water and pour it into the filter manually. There is still a great brewer on the market today which uses this method: The Chemex.

In 1936, a German citizen, by the name of Dr. Peter Schlumbohm, immigrated to the United States. With him he brought a concept for a new type of coffee brewer. His idea was to use a heavier paper filter that would absorb more of the oils and, perhaps, impurities that a regular pour over would not. The chemist pursued his dream and, in 1941, obtained a patent on his brewer, The Chemex. Due to the heavier, more absorbent paper, the resulting coffee was definitely cleaner, and much brighter, in the cup. His brewer requires a coarser grind. This is how it works:

The glass brewer looks like two triangles inverted on top of each other. A heavy cone shaped paper filter is inserted directly into the space between the triangles. The thickness of the filter allows water to pass through the grounds in the upper chamber and through into the lower chamber. A regular paper filter would not withstand this pressure, and would break.

Brewing with a Chemex

-use a coarser (not fine, grind of coffee)

-insert the Chemex paper filter into your brewer. The filter, when opened, has a side that is one layer in thickness, and a side that is three layers in thickness. The three layer side of paper should be facing the spout of the pot.

- add your coffee. Chemex recommends a tbsp per 5 oz cup, however, again, as with a filter drip machine the measurements are a personal choice.

-now boil water, and let it stand 15-30 seconds before pouring. The reason this is important is that water at the boil will actually burn the coffee grounds, resulting in a bitter brew.

-on your first pour, just allow a small amount of water to contact the coffee grounds. The hot water will push the ground coffee upward, this is called a bloom. The bloom releases all of the essence of the coffee, and prepares it for the remaining brewing process.

-continue to pour the hot water over the coffee grounds, being careful to keep the water level below ¾ of the height of the filter.

–it will take some time, and several pour over's.

–the end result is a considerably less cloudy, cleaner tasting brew.

Some people admire the Chemex, and keep their brewed coffee on a hot plate on the table while serving company. This is quite acceptable, however, be sure to make the brewing process part of the presentation, and serve coffee directly upon completion- the burner will burn your brew. And remember- never put your Chemex on a stove top burner!

Although conceived in the late 1930's, the Chemex is still a unique, and eye appealing brewer. Need more information? Visit Chemexcoffeemaker.com.

On the opposite end of this spectrum comes a brewer which strives to go in a completely opposite direction. Its name? The Bodum, sometimes called the French press, or cafetierre.

1958, Copenhagen, Denmark

Peter Bodum introduces the Bodum Santos vacuum brewing system.

He strives to extract as much of the oils and sediments as possible, for a heavier, more complex cup. His creation, which you can still buy today works like this:

Cold water is poured into the bottom glass chamber, Coarsely ground coffee is placed in the top glass chamber. A glass funnel tube connects the two. The bottom chamber is put over heat, soon causing a vacuum. The vacuum forces the heated water up the tube into the ground coffee. Unlike drip coffee, the grounds and the water stay in contact longer, causing more extraction. When all of the hot water has entered the top chamber and combined with the ground coffee, the pot is taken off the heat source. As the bottom chamber cools, the coffee is vacuumed back down. You can now remove the top glass chamber and pour your brew. This brewer is definitely a conversation piece. Awe your houseguests, however if you purchase one, be careful! It is delicate.

In 1974, Peter's son, Joergen Bodum, introduces the first 'Press Pot.'

Everyone has their favorite method of brewing coffee-this is mine. Again, as with his father's vacuum pot, the Press Pot is designed for more extraction due to the length of time the ground coffee and hot water stay in contact. You will be extracting all of the coffee's essence, oils, and, yes, some sediment. This is how it works:

Coarsely ground coffee is put directly into the bottom of the French Press. Bodum recommends 1 scoop of coffee per 4 oz cup. When you purchase a Bodum, you should receive a measuring scoop. Always use this scoop with your press. Again, the ratio of ground coffee to water is a personal choice. Boil water, let it stand 15-30 seconds. Pour water directly over grounds, filling to one inch of top of the beaker. Stir the mixture with a plastic utensil. (If you use any utensil other than plastic, you can scratch the glass beaker and risk breakage.) Baby your Bodum! Let  coffee mixture extract 4-5 minutes. There is a reusable filter screen attached to the Bodum's lid. Insert the filter and lid into the top of the Bodum. Now firmly and slowly 'press' the filter to the bottom. The coffee grounds are forced to the bottom, leaving your fresh brew on top. Now simply pour your freshly brewed coffee into a cup, and enjoy! The result, again, is heavy, thick, and somewhat grainy, definitely coffee!

TIP: If you are enjoying coffee with someone who enjoys a less intense brew, depending on the size of your Bodum, press the filter ¼ to ½ way after half the brewing time and pour their cup. The coffee's oils adhere to the screen's reusable filter, ensuring your heavier brew will remain in the bottom of the Bodum to keep extracting. Keep it Clean—

I loosen my Bodum's filter screen and thoroughly rinse it after every use. I recommend taking the screen totally apart weekly and washing the separate pieces--they are all dishwasher safe. Replacement screens, and replacement carafes, for that matter, are available.

For more information, visit Bodum.com

Now, for something completely different! A coffee brewer that implements cold water. Cold water ensures a cup that is very low in acidity--perfect for anyone with a delicate stomach. The great thing about the coffee that this brewer produces is its versatility.

Timeline—Early 1960's.   Location—Guatemala

An American garden nursery owner is looking to expand his inventory. Taking a break for a cup of joe, he is presented with a pot of hot water and a carafe of what he finds out is a cold water coffee concentrate. His name--

Todd Simpson. Todd's wife has a delicate stomach. Todd decides to pursue a brew his wife can consume; the result, named after him--the Toddy Maker. How does it work?

A durable plastic container, equipped with a reusable filter in the bottom, is filled with one pound of coarsely ground Under the filter is a rubber cork to keep the water in. Pour cold water directly over the coffee grounds, filling to the top of the plastic container. Let the cold water and ground coffee slurry sit at room temperature for a minimum of 12 hours, then, pull the cork! The coffee  concentrate filters into the accompanying glass carafe.

Kudos: The concentrate is definitely less acidic and very mellow. In fact, it is up to 67% less acidic. Super smooth. It can be made hot or cold. Using a ratio of ⅓ concentrate to ⅔ hot water, it makes 'instant' coffee that's not really instant! ⅓ concentrate combined with ⅔ cold milk makes an extraordinary iced coffee. Use espresso roast coffee to make awesome iced cafe mochas, etc. Look for my recipes in the cold drink recipe sections of the book. The concentrate will stay fresh in your refrigerator up to three weeks and can also be frozen. Tip…when I was managing a coffee shop in Sarasota, Florida, a woman who was an avid gardener asked if we would save all of our used coffee grounds for her. She would pick up 6 ten gallon containers of grounds every week. Her home was only one block away. One day I drove by her house and was awed by her flowers and vast array of plants. It appears that coffee grounds make excellent fertilizer. Is it only me who finds it a coincidence that a garden nursery owner is even now contributing to house and garden plants? Use left over Toddy grounds to fertilize your house plants or garden. You will notice a remarkable difference. For more information, visit Toddycafe.com. I'm all coffee'd out!!

Espresso yourself!

Ahh . . . espresso . . . the coffee lover's elixir. Elixer--no other word can suffice!

Taken from the early Arabic term 'al-iks-Ir' it literally means remedy, or cure all. Can you relate? Only the most indulgent coffee fans can appreciate the purism of the act of partaking in a freshly pulled shot of espresso. It trickles out of the portafilter like honey, filling a demitasse cup with ¾-1 ½ ounces of liquid gold topped with a velvety crown of crema. It is meant to be savored. Remember these three words: savor the moment.

Straight espresso reacts quickly to oxygen, and is meant to be consumed immediately after brewing. A moment in time. Coffee lover's nirvana. But I digress...

Timeline–1800'S   Location–France

The quest for the perfect espresso is being pursued in earnest. Countless brewing contraptions are being experimented with. Enter Louis Bernard Babaut, circa 1822. A breakthrough in coffee history is about to begin. Babaut creates a machine which utilizes steam and pressure to force hot water through a filter filled with finely ground dark roasted coffee. The machine is very temperamental and prone to blowing up. This is due to the extreme pressure it produces. However, this does not stop a gentleman, by the name of Edward Loysel deSantais, who commercializes the machine and debuts it at the Paris Exposition in 1855. The machine was said to produce up to 1,000 demitasse cups of espresso coffee an hour . . . a lot of satisfied customers, and we are still lining up today.

There are two ways to produce your favorite espresso based coffee house drinks at home. The first machine is actually an upgraded version of Babaut's original which relies on steam and pressure. A steam/pressure based espresso machine is perfect for the novice to learn the concepts of brewing an espresso, and also to practice the technique of steaming milk for specialty drinks. You will soon find out if you want to pursue your passion and upgrade to the next level. A steam based machine creates enough pressure to make one or two espressos at a time, and also allows you to steam your milk. The milk must be steamed simultaneously. You have to utilize the limited amount of water in the reservoir. Once you have brewed your espresso and steamed your milk, you must let any remaining pressurized steam escape from the steam wand before refilling the water reservoir to start over again. If you only want to brew drinks for one or two people, this may be perfect for you. The second version, which produces a much better quality end product, is the pump machine. A pump machine does the work for you. The pump takes the water from the reservoir through a heating element (thermal block) to the brew head and steam wand. It separates the functions of brewing espresso and steaming milk, so you can just brew an espresso, or just steam milk, or do both simultaneously. The pressure is even and contained. Both machines work on the same principal, taking cold water, heating it to at least 190 degrees F, and then forcing the heated water through a portafilter containing finely ground espresso roast coffee. The end result is a combination of all of the above: the water temperature (important!), the amount of pressure and, most importantly of all, the grind of the coffee. The following are examples of a pressure based, and a pump driven machine.

I strive for perfection when brewing my espresso. Being the coffee hound that I am, I want nothing less than a perfect cup. To achieve this, I know that the best way to go is to spend a little more money and purchase a burr grinder and a pump machine. Why?

A burr grinder ensures a more consistent grind. A blade grinder 'chops' the coffee beans. Some of the pieces will be larger; some of the pieces will be smaller. This will result in the larger pieces being under-extracted and the smaller pieces over-extracted, resulting in a defective cup. When you use a burr grinder, the coffee beans are passed through the rotating burr blades only once. Each bean is ground to the same uniform size. When the heated water is forced through the ground espresso coffee, each grain releases the same amount of essence, oil, flavor, and aroma. The perfect balance. The perfect demitasse cup.

A pump machine produces much more pressure creating better extraction. Crema, the sign of a perfect espresso, is obtained. As long as you have water in the reservoir, you can steam milk all the day long. It can be heated up and ready for use in very little time simply by pressing the on/off switch. These facts, combined with the convenience, win me over. Plug it in. Fill the reservoir with fresh water. Retrieve your faithful grinder. Indulge in the ritual. Espresso yourself!

'Pulling' a shot of espresso

Begin by placing the insertable filter into the portafilter. Fill the filter up to ¾ with finely ground espresso coffee. Shake the portafilter lightly to distribute the ground coffee evenly. Next, 'tamp' the coffee. Some pump machines are equipped with a built in tamper, others require a manual tamp. The purpose of tamping is to ensure an even surface for the heated water to flow through. The even surface, combined with the proper grind, ensures ultimate extraction. Place the tamper onto the ground coffee in the portafilter. Apply an even pressure and firmly press the tamper into the portafilter. The coffee is compressed into the filter. The grind of the coffee, combined with tamping, will both be major factors in your shot of espresso. You will find your own personal style of tamp by practice–some do a straight up tamp, some 'polish' the tamp by twisting the tamper on the coffees surface. Either way, you want that even surface. Once tamped, be sure that the rim of the portafilter is free of coffee grounds. Wipe the rims surface with your hand to ensure this. The reason this is important is that there is a rubber gasket on the brew head which has direct contact with the portafilter's rim–this creates a seal which allows the pressurized hot water to obtain optimal extraction of the ground coffee. Take the portafilter and, starting on the left hand side of the group (or brew) head, find the place where it fits. Now slide the portafilter to the right until it feels firm–don't over tighten. You are now ready to pull a shot of espresso. If everything has been done properly: freshly filtered water, freshly ground espresso roast coffee, the proper grind and tamping, you are golden! Close your eyes and inhale . . . experience the moment . . . but don't wait too long--your precious brew is awaiting! It is the perfect combination of all your efforts--enjoy it!

Whether you grind your own coffee at home or have your favorite coffee house grind it for you, find the right grind. Invest in a kitchen timer. A perfect shot of espresso should be at 190 - 200 degrees and will take 17-24 seconds to pull. The grind and tamp will assure this time line. The espresso will flow slowly, in a honey like consistency. The sign that you have achieved your quest is the crema, a golden foam floating on the top of the brew. Coffee contains natural oils, some soluble that dissolve in water, some non soluble, which don't dissolve. The crema is made up of the non soluble oils and makes the perfect espresso shot perfect!

There are many ways to utilize espresso, but the three most well known drinks are the cappuccino, the latté, and the café mocha. They all share two basic components: espresso coffee and steamed milk. The combination of the two is enjoyed by millions of people every day. Steaming the milk is the major taste factor in all specialty coffee drinks. The act of steaming the milk alters its chemistry, sweetening it.

What you will need to create your drinks are: a stainless steel steaming pitcher, a kitchen thermometer, and a lot of practice. First the milk. Remember this: the colder the milk and the lower the fat content, the better froth you will obtain. So, cold skim milk makes the best froth. Here is a great tip: keep your steaming pitcher in the refrigerator or freezer.

To froth the milk, add milk to the pitcher until just below half full. (The milk will expand.) Place the thermometer in the milk. Before placing the steaming wand in the pitcher, open it to let out any moisture that may be in the line. Now, place the steam wand in the milk, just beneath the surface, and open. The steam will expand and froth the milk. This takes some practice; too deep and you will have no froth, too close to the surface and you will get large, wet bubbles. I call the right spot to be the 'happy place.' Listen! You can actually hear the happy place. Continue to steam and froth the milk until it reaches a temperature of 160 degrees F. Turn off steam wand and set the pitcher aside for 30 seconds or more. This will allow the milk to condense and give you a more luxuriant froth. It also gives you time to wipe the milk off of the steam wand and open it to blow out any milk that may have accumulated inside. Keep it clean!

Some espresso machines come with an alternative to manually steaming your milk--an automatic frother. The device attaches to the steaming wand, and utilizes the pressure produced by the steam to automatically produce frothed milk. Goof proof. I prefer to steam my milk manually–old school. Again, it's based on your personal preference.

Now that you have the knowledge, I will give you some measurements of coffee to milk. These are my preferences; there is a great debate about how much froth is on a cappuccino or latte. Do what works for you and enjoy!

Cappuccino   Roughly, ⅓ espresso, ⅓ steamed milk and ⅓ frothed milk

Café Latte   ⅓ espresso, ⅔ steamed milk with very little or no froth

Café Mocha   ⅓ espresso, ⅔ steamed milk, liquid chocolate, whipped cream (some people steam chocolate milk)

ESPRESSO LINGO

Shot sizes	single..one shot, double..two shots, triple..three shots quad.. four shots, ristretto (restricted), or short, doppio (double), lungo (long)
Con Panna	with whipped cream
Romano	with a twist of lemon
Macchiato	*'marked'* or topped with a spoonful of frothed milk
Americano	⅓ espresso, ⅔ hot water
Shot in the dark (aka red eye)	an espresso shot in a regular cup of coffee
Tall	Regular Size
Grande	Large Size
Half Caff	AAAAAHHHHH!!! ½ Regular ½ Decaf coffee
Skinny	Made with skim milk
Whipless, Or Naked	with no froth or whipped cream

Breve   Any specialty espresso based
                          drink substituted with half
                          and half cream instead of milk

You figure it out. "I want a double, tall, whipless, half caff, breve, café mocha, please!"

How Frasier Crane!

Did you know?

- Achilles Gaggia perfected the first espresso pump machine in Italy in 1938. The Gaggia machine can still be found in thousands of homes and coffee houses world wide.
- Three years before Gaggia's accomplishment, another Italian, Alfonso Bialetti, created the first aluminum stove top espresso maker. It was such a hit it is estimated it was in 90% of all Italian homes and made the Guinness Book of World Records.
- The term Americano is thought to have come from US soldiers in World War II France. They would dilute their espresso with hot water to obtain a strength more comparable to American taste. The French would scoff, "Ahh! Americanos!"
- It takes approximately 41 coffee beans to make a shot of espresso.
- Coffee beans contain natural oils. When roasted, the oils are forced to the bean's surface. Caffeine, which is contained in the oil, is also forced out. The darker the roast is, the less caffeine the bean contains.

So . . . espresso roast coffee contains LESS caffeine!

8 oz. coffee	85 milligrams of caffeine
1 ½ oz. espresso shot	65 milligrams of caffeine

I know that you now have enough knowledge to confidently prepare your own café quality espresso based drinks at home. The next portion of Celebrating the Bean explores different ways to utilize both espresso and regular brewed coffee in many ways. With your copy of Celebrating the Bean in hand, head to the hub of your home. Plug it in. Fill the reservoir with fresh water. Retrieve your faithful grinder. Celebrate…

Picture this . . . an old time diner. Heavy white porcelain cups. A sassy waitress dressed in a white-and-pink striped dress. A morning ritual. Friends and conversation. Comfort food. Good coffee. A slice of Americana. Canadiana. Italiano. Mexicano. It's Coffee.

The celebrated bean is universal. Different cultures not only use different brewing techniques but original ways of utilizing coffee, not only in beverages and desserts, even in entrees. In the following chapters, you will find some truly remarkable recipes. Some were submitted to me via e-mail, some personally. Others I wrote myself or have accumulated over the years as I pursued my passion. If you have your nose in this book, you are obviously a coffee fan as well.

Raise a mug of your favorite brew, as we all salute   T H E C E L E B R A T E D   B E A N ! !

My original concept when writing Celebrating the Bean was to have every recipe in the book submitted to me by fellow coffee lovers. I aspired to have submissions from people worldwide, having the entire recipe section contributed. I found however, that trying to get people to give you their recipe is like pulling teeth. The first step I took was to set up an e-mail account where coffee lovers could submit their recipes. I started by advertising with fliers at a local hospital. They were posted on every bulletin board in every department, including all public boards. Think about how long you sometimes wait in the emergency room with ample time on your hands. Any reading material would surely be of significance. I simply asked for a recipe, a name, and a city. From yourself, or any family members or friends, locally or globally. In exchange, I would put your recipe, name, and city in my book. I also had a copy of my flier published in a sister hospital's newsletter, and featured on the front page of a community website. One week, no response. Two weeks, no response. One month, no response. I thought, "maybe people don't read…?" I tried another alternative: the flier's remained posted, mind you. I now joined a free online forum that is based entirely on coffee. I gave myself the alias "two beans". I shared my plight with thousands of other coffee lovers. I asked these coffee hounds to send me their recipes. The result, you may well ask? The last time I checked, I had 374 hits on my post; I got three responses. I can feel a little blood trickling from my left ear as my head feels like it is about to explode. I'm frustrated. I was sure that I would be inundated with recipes. Then, Michelle and Yvonne, the marketing team at the hospital, approach me with an idea that will surely gain results. They have ties with a local radio show. Radio WIBQ a.m., Sarasota, Fl. The show is an hour in length; however four guests are scheduled, so each can get their 15 minutes of fame. I'm now on the airwaves--a little nervous and with a somewhat shaky voice, albeit. I ply my plight again, this time live. I'm sure the listeners will feel my pain and respond in accordance. Uh uh. I try family members, have friends put me on their e-mail lists, tell everybody I see about the concept, and I finally do get a response, although not what I anticipated. The people that responded were meant to join me in my journey through life. Their input means a lot to me and I would like to give them all a mighty 'Thank You' from the very soul of my being. These are their recipes--please enjoy them... 'two beans.'

Submitted Recipes

These were the very first recipes submitted to me. They came from a major coffee lover, a rival.

Seattle's Signature Steak

$33.95 for dinner at a popular Seattle eatery, served with special saltwater sourdough bread, seasonal vegetables, and your choice of a baked potato, hash browns, mashed potatoes, or fries, $8.36 at home

12oz	Filet mignon--$6.36
3Tbsp.	ground espresso--$.55
1cup	Cabernet Sauvignon--$1.35
1tsp.	Kosher salt--$.02
⅛tsp.	onion powder--$.02
⅛tsp.	garlic powder--$.01
⅛tsp.	black pepper--$.03
⅛tsp.	cayenne pepper--$.01
1 pinch	paprika--$.01

Prepare steak for cooking:

Start by trimming any fat away from the edges of the filet. Cover with plastic wrap and use mallet to hammer into 1-inch thickness. Using a small, shallow bowl; submerse fillet in 1 cup of Cabernet Sauvignon for several hours. Cabernet Sauvignon is a dry red wine found in most package stores and supermarkets. In a separate bowl, combine the remaining dry ingredients including the ground espresso. After the steak has marinated, place into bowl with dry spices and espresso, then coat liberally.

Grilling steak:

Grill each side of filet on high heat for 3 minutes. High heat will create flames with most home grills. Decrease, or move, from high heat and continue cooking until desired temperature is reached. Filet mignon is best served medium rare, which measures 130- 140 degrees internal temperature. If you don't have a thermometer, cook steak for an additional 10 to12 minutes.

Accompany this flavorful steak with a vegetable and starch of your desire.

Judith Reynal, St. Petersburg,Florida

Red Eye Gravy

As taught to me by my Grandmother, Ophelia Greer Skipworth (b. 1882 d. 1972) circa 1964

Take a well seasoned cast iron skillet. Take a goodly slice of country cured ham (ex, Smithfield). Make sure that the ham has a least a ¼ inch of fat on it. Heat the skillet 'til it's hot. Fry up the ham 'til it is browned and has rendered its fat. Put the ham on a plate. Throw a cup of hot coffee in the hot skillet and cook it down, making sure that you scrape up all the browned bits of ham that stuck to the skillet. Serve with ham and grits or biscuits.

Translation: Do NOT use a non stick skillet--not good for the crispy brown parts. My grandmother's coffee cup held about 7 ounces of coffee. This measurement is not exact by any means. If you use modern day (non country cured) ham, make sure that all of the water that cooks out is evaporated before you add the coffee. 'cook it down'-- reduce by ⅓

Judith Reynal, St. Petersburg, Florida

My second submission…

Café au Lait or Café con Leche

1 cup strong dark roast gourmet coffee or espresso
1 cup hot milk

No, Starbucks was not the first to serve au lait in the U.S. in the 1980s. Cubans have been serving café con leche for decades down in Miami. Anyway, this traditional Spanish and French drink is prepared by simultaneously pouring equal amounts of hot, strong dark roast gourmet coffee and hot milk into a large cup. The milk can either be heated in the microwave or stovetop. The heated milk adds a special sweetness to this delicious drink. The Cuban version is actually prepared with a cup of hot milk and a shot of Cuban coffee poured into it. Sugar is a must to fully appreciate this drink. Makes 2 servings.

Buck Contreras, owner, Volcanicacoffee.com

Contributed to me on an online coffee forum. Check out Buck's awesome website--he is a fellow Costa Rican coffee fan.

My third submission...

Brazilian Chocolate Coffee

Ingredients
 2 cups hot chocolate
 1 cup hot coffee
 ½ cup milk
 2 tbsp powdered sugar

2 scoops vanilla or chocolate ice cream
whipped cream

Step by step
mix all the ingredients in sauce pan
heat until bubbling
serve in mugs with whipped cream

**By Chris Reddy, Kitchener, Ontario, Canada
(A teenage coffee fan)**
The following recipes, in the order I received them, were submitted to me personally or were submitted to me by e-mail via my e-mail account.

Kahlua & Crème de Cocoa Cake

1 box deep chocolate cake mix
1 4 ½ oz instant chocolate pudding mix
4 eggs at room temperature
½ cup oil
¾ c strong coffee (cooled)
¾ cup Kahlua & Crème de Cocoa combined

Combine liquid and dry ingredients and mix
for four minutes (medium to high speed)

Pour into a greased and floured bundt pan and
bake for 45 to 50 minutes in a 350 degree oven.

Glaze

Combine
1 cup sifted confectionary sugar
2 Tablespoons strong coffee (cooled)
2 Tablespoons Kahlua
2 Tablespoons Crème de Cocoa

Mix until smooth consistency.

Poke holes with a two pronged fork (meat fork) into the top of the cooled cake and drizzle the glaze over the cake.
Adriane Donley, Trumansburg, NY

Brazilian Coffee Ice Cream

Start with custard based ice cream as follows:
6 egg yolks (room temperature)
1 ⅓ cups sugar
1 quart light cream or half and half
¼ teaspoon salt
⅓ cup instant freeze dried coffee dissolved
in 3 tablespoons hot water (cooled)
1 tablespoon vanilla extract
2 cups heavy cream

Beat egg yolks slightly in the top of a double boiler and stir in sugar, light cream, and salt. Place over simmering water and stirring constantly, cook until custard coats the spoon. Remove from heat and stir in vanilla extract, dissolved freeze dried coffee and heavy cream. Chill. Freeze as directed in one gallon size ice cream freezer.

While ice cream is freezing, finely chop 1 cup Brazil nuts and sauté in 1 tablespoon butter until golden brown. Cool. Place ½ pound semisweet chocolate, ½ cup heavy cream and ⅓ light corn syrup in the top of a double boiler. Heat over simmering water, stirring until smoothly blended. To serve, spoon ice cream into dessert bowls, drizzle with chocolate sauce, and sprinkle with toasted nuts. Serves 8
Adriane Donley, Trumansburg, NY

Bernice Griffith

Bernice's recipe for coffee starts with freshly grown & brewed coffee from Grenada. Bernice tells the story of growing up in the West Indies on the Caribbean island of Grenada where an 8 ounce cup of coffee also meant adding a tablespoon of brown sugar, a pinch of cinnamon or nutmeg and good conversations with family and friends.
Bernice currently resides in Sarasota, Florida but continues to enjoy the flavors of home.
(Contributed by a good friend of Bernice, Corista Williams, who resides in Lakewood Ranch, Florida)

Easy Coffee Chocolate Mousse

Ingredients needed:
2 quarts heavy whipping cream
½ cup chocolate syrup
1 tablespoon general foods international gourmet coffee (powder)

Method of Prep:
Whip cream until stiff. Add in chocolate syrup and coffee. Mix until well blended.
Serving suggestion: serve in coffee cups, garnish with cocoa powder or confectioners sugar. Top cake or cupcakes with mousse. Fill a graham cracker crust (pie shell) with this mixture and serve as a refrigerated pie.
Tim Schoonmaker, Brandon, Fl

Coffee Infused Sweet Chicken Breast

Ingredients needed:
Chicken breasts
 Coffee, brewed strong, about 2 cups worth
1 tablespoon cinnamon
1 tablespoon nutmeg
4 whole cloves
1 onion diced
1 pepper, diced
salt and pepper to taste
olive oil for sautéing

Method of Prep: Using the coffee, in a plastic bag, mix coffee, cinnamon, nutmeg, and cloves together. Add chicken and let sit for about 20 minutes. In a sauté pan, using a little oil, sauté the onions and peppers until tender. Remove chicken from bag and sauté with the onions and peppers. Use the salt and pepper to taste. Add any other seasonings you wish.

Tim Schoonmaker, Brandon, Fl

Espresso Brownies

2 C sugar

3 large eggs

15 T unsalted butter

1 ½ t vanilla extract

¾ C unsweetened cocoa powder

1 ¼ flour

3 T finely ground espresso or Jamaican coffee

½ t salt

¾ chopped pecans

6 T freshly brewed espresso or Jamaican coffee

1 C bittersweet or semi sweet chocolate chips

Preheat oven to 350 degrees. Spray 13 x9 x2 metal pan with vegetable oil spray. Soften butter in microwave. Combine sugar, butter, cocoa, ground coffee and salt in large bowl and mix until blended. Texture will be grainy. Whisk in eggs and vanilla. Fold in flour. Mix in pecans. Spread in prepared pan and bake about 25 minutes or until pick in center comes out clean. Brew fresh espresso or coffee and mix the 6 tablespoons with the 6 oz (1 cup) chocolate chips until smooth. Let ganache stand 1 hour. Spread evenly over brownies. Let stand at room temperature. May be made 1 day ahead.

Denise Salomon , Bradenton, Fl
(Manatee Memorial Hospital)

Orange Iced Coffee

Juice of 2 oranges
2 oranges peeled (save peel and cut into pieces)
1 cup sugar or to taste
4-6 cups of cold coffee
whipped cream
crushed ice

Place orange peel, water and sugar into saucepan bring to a boil and boil for 5 minutes
Combine orange juice, syrup and coffee add whipped cream. Pour over crushed ice in a tall glass. Garnish with orange zest or an orange slice
* For an extra treat add a shot of Grand Marnier per glass (yeah,baby!)

John and Colleen Knechtel, Kitchener,
Ontario, Canada

Chocolate Roll

6 eggs, separated
½ cup sugar
6 ounces semi sweet chocolate chips
3 Tablespoons strong coffee
1 teaspoon vanilla
Cocoa
Confectioners' sugar
1 ½ cups heavy cream, whipped and sweetened

Butter an 11 X 14 X 1 pan; line it with waxed paper and butter the paper. Beat the egg yolks until light and lemon colored; gradually beat in the sugar. Melt the chocolate with coffee in the top of a double boiler. Let cool slightly, and then add to egg yolks. Beat well. Beat in vanilla. Beat the egg whites until stiff enough to form peaks (but do not beat dry). Fold into the chocolate mixture. Pour batter into the prepared pan, spreading evenly. Bake in a 350 degree oven for 15 minutes or until a knife inserted into the center comes out clean. Remove from the oven; cover with a damp towel and let stand for about 20 minutes. Tear an 18 inch length of waxed paper and place on work area; sprinkle with cocoa and confectioner's sugar. Run a spatula around the edges of the cake and invert on the waxed paper; it should turn out easily. Carefully remove the paper on which it was baked. Spread the cake with sweetened whipped cream. Then, by lifting the edge of the waxed paper under the cake, get the long end of the cake to fold inward; this starts the cake rolling. Continue lifting the waxed paper and roll up the cake gently and quickly onto a large platter. Serves 8 to 10.

Devra Cohen, Falls Church, Virginia

La Patisserie Mousse Au Chocolat

8 oz. semi-sweet chocolate bits
1 tsp. instant coffee
1 tsp. boiling water
6 eggs, separated and at room temp.
3 tbsp. Sugar
2 cups heavy cream, well chilled

Place chocolate in top of double-boiler and melt over simmering water. Dissolve instant coffee in boiling water and set aside to cool. Add egg yolks to melted chocolate, one at a time, and stir until smooth. Beat egg whites until soft peaks form. Fold in sugar and beat until stiff but not dry. Stir about ¼ of the whites into the chocolate mixture and then gently fold in the rest. Chill while preparing whipped cream. Using a chilled bowl and chilled bowl and chilled beaters, whip the cream until softly peaked, not stiff. Add the coffee. Fold whipped cream into chocolate mixture. Spoon mousse into a 2½-3 quart serving bowl or soufflé dish and chill at least 6 hrs or overnight.
Yield: 12 servings. (Recipe may be cut in half)

Cake Form

Line the sides of a 9 or 10 inch spring form pan (2½ to 3" deep) with split ladyfingers placed vertically. You will need about 2½ dozen split ladyfingers. Fit a ½ inch thick circle of plain yellow sponge cake tightly into the bottom of the pan. Fill with the mousse and refrigerate or freeze until firm. Unmold before serving.

Note: The mousse may also be made in advance and frozen. If it is served frozen, it will have an ice cream consistency. It may be thawed in the refrigerator for several hours before serving.

Anita A. Sabato, Lakewood Ranch, FL

Praline Cheesecake

1 ¼ Cups crushed graham crackers (18 square crackers)
¼ cup granulated sugar
¼ cup chopped pecans, toasted
¼ cup butter or margarine, melted
3 8-ounce packages cream cheese, softened
1 cup packed brown sugar
1 5 ⅓ -ounce can (⅔ cup) evaporated milk
½ cup strong-brewed Coffee, cooled
3 Tablespoons all purpose flour
1 ½ teaspoons vanilla
3 eggs
1 cup pecan halves
½ cup light corn syrup
½ cup strong brewed coffee
2 Tablespoons cornstarch
1 Tablespoon brown sugar
½ teaspoon vanilla

Combine cracker crumbs, the granulated sugar, and the chopped pecans. Stir in butter or margarine. Press mixture over bottom and 1 ½ inches up the sides of a 9 inch spring form pan. Bake in 350 degree oven for 10 minutes. Cool on wire rack. Meanwhile, beat together cream cheese, the 1 cup brown sugar, the evaporated milk, the ½ cup coffee, the flour, and the 1 ½ teaspoons vanilla. Add eggs; beat just until blended. Pour into baked crust. Bake in 350 degree oven for 50 to 55 minutes or until set. Cool in pan 30 minutes; loosen sides and remove rim from pan. Cool. Arrange pecan halves atop. Chill several hours or overnight. In saucepan, combine corn syrup, the ½ cup coffee, the corn starch, and the remaining brown sugar. Cook, stirring constantly, until thickened and bubbly. Remove from heat; stir in the remaining vanilla. Cool slightly. Serve with cheesecake. Makes 12 to 16 servings.

Susan Schussler, Sarasota, Fl

Ice Cream Delight

Fill a bowl with your choice of ice cream then sprinkle 3-4 finely ground coffee beans on top.
Also try adding walnuts, pecans or even macadamia along with the coffee

Catherine Schmidt St. Jacobs, Ontario, Canada

Almond Coffee Refrigerator Cake

1 c. butter
1 ½ c. powdered sugar
2 egg yolks, well beaten
½ c. cold strong coffee
⅛ tsp. salt
1 tsp. vanilla
½ c. chopped, toasted almonds
18-20 ladyfingers, split
Whipped cream

Cream butter in mixing bowl. Add sugar gradually. Add egg yolks, beat until smooth and fluffy. Add coffee, small amount at a time, mixing well after each addition. Add salt, vanilla and almonds; mix well.

Line loaf pan with waxed paper. Cover bottom of pan with ladyfinger halves, flat side down. Spread ½ coffee mixture over ladyfingers; cover with layer of ladyfingers. Add remaining coffee mixture, then layer of ladyfingers. Chill for at least 4 hours. Turn out on small platter. Garnish with whipped cream

Amanda Hartman, Tampa Fl
(I call her 'Little Amanda' or L.A. for short)

twobeans

Here is my original recipe for Rocky Mocha Road Brownies. They are Very Good!

Brownie Ingredients:

¾ C Flour
½ tsp. Baking Powder
½ tsp. Salt
1 Egg
1 C. Sugar
2 oz. Baking Chocolate
½ C. Butter
¼ C. double-strength coffee
½ C. Pecans, broken into pieces

For the topping:

1 C. Miniature Marshmallows
½ C. chopped Pecans
½ C. butterscotch chips
½ C. semi-sweet chocolate chips

Mix dry ingredients and set aside. Beat eggs in bowl for 1 minute. Add sugar and continue beating for another 1 minute. Melt Baking Chocolate and Butter over double boiler, or microwave to melt. Let chocolate mixture cool slightly, then add powdered coffee to mixture. Add chocolate/butter/coffee mixture to egg and sugar mixture in bowl. Add flour mixture and broken pecans to bowl, stirring. Pour mixture into greased 8" square pan. Bake at 350° for 20-25 minutes, or until barely done. Insert wooden toothpick in center to test - if toothpick comes out clean, the brownies are done.

Do not turn off oven! Immediately sprinkle all topping ingredients over top of brownies as soon as you remove them from oven. Return to oven for 3 minutes, or until chocolate chips are soft. Tip: have all topping ingredients mixed together in a bowl before removing brownies from oven to enable you to add to brownies quickly before the brownies cool. Cut with knife dipped in hot water. Makes 16 brownies.

From the kitchen of The Beanery Roasting Co. Ellen
www.thebeanery.com

My final submission, received one week before the first finished rough draft of my book went to the publisher...

Short Ribs Braised in Coffee Ancho Chile Sauce

Recipe by Chef Tommy Klauber of Pattigeorge's Restaurant Longboat Key, Florida

4 dried ancho chiles, stemmed, seeded, and ribs discarded
2 cups boiling-hot water
1 medium onion, quartered
3 garlic cloves, coarsely chopped
2 tablespoons finely chopped canned chipotle chiles in adobo plus 2 teaspoons adobo sauce
2 tablespoons pure maple syrup

1 tablespoon fresh lime juice
3 teaspoons salt
6 lb beef short ribs
1 teaspoon black pepper
1 tablespoon vegetable oil
½ cup brewed coffee

Preheat oven to 350°F.

Soak ancho chiles in boiling-hot water until softened, about 20 minutes, and then drain in a colander set over a bowl. Taste soaking liquid: It will be a little bitter, but if unpleasantly so, discard it; otherwise, reserve for braising. Transfer ancho chilies to a blender and purée with onion, garlic, chipotles with sauce, maple syrup, lime juice, and 1 teaspoon salt.

Pat ribs dry and sprinkle with pepper and remaining 2 teaspoons salt. Heat oil in a 12 inch heavy skillet over moderately high heat until hot but not smoking, then brown ribs in 3 batches, turning occasionally, about 5 minutes per batch. Transfer as browned to a roasting pan just large enough to hold ribs in 1 layer.

Carefully add chile purée to fat remaining in skillet (use caution, since it will splatter and steam) and cook over moderately low heat, stirring frequently, 5 minutes. Add reserved chile soaking liquid (or 1 ½ cups water) and coffee and bring to a boil, then pour over ribs (liquid should come about halfway up sides of meat).

Cover roasting pan tightly with foil and braise ribs in middle of oven until very tender, 3 to 3 ½ hours. Skim fat from pan juices and serve with ribs.

Chefs' note: Ribs improve in flavor if braised 2 days ahead. Cool, uncovered, then chill, surface covered with parchment paper or wax paper and roasting pan covered with foil. Remove any solidified fat before reheating. Makes 6 servings.

Submitted by Sheryl Vieira President of Marketing & PR Mark P. Riley Luxury Real Estate Group Sarasota, FL 34240

Again thank you to all recipe submitters…

It's a family affair.

Of course my family responded to my request; after all I was raised in a coffee environment and they felt my pain. These are their contributions…from old to young alike.

Coffee Pot Roast

2 tbsp butter
4 lb chuck roast
1 tbsp butter (2nd amount)
Salt to taste
1 onion chopped
6 cups brewed coffee
2 cups sliced mushrooms
3 tbsp cornstarch

Sear meat and remove from pan, then add remaining butter, salt, and onion sauté 4 to 5 minutes. Return meat to pan and add coffee and mushrooms. Bring to a boil and reduce heat and simmer for 5-5 ½ hours

Gravy

Using liquid from pan stir in cornstarch until smooth and whisk into pan Will make 6-8 servings

Clifford Stockdale (my father) Kitchener Ontario Canada

Spaghetti Sauce

1 lb pound ground ½ cup sliced mushrooms
½ cup onion chopped
½ cup green pepper chopped
2 cloves minced garlic
½ teaspoon salt
1 cup brewed coffee
2 16 oz cans stewed tomatoes
1 oz can tomato sauce
1 bay leaf
1 tsp sugar
Basil, thyme, oregano to taste

Brown meat, mushrooms, onions, peppers and garlic in large pot, drain fat. Add remaining ingredients; bring to a boil and lower heat. Simmer to desired consistency. Serve over your favorite pasta.

Irene Stockdale (my mother)Kitchener, Ontario Canada

Chicken with Cardamom & Coffee

8 tbsp finely ground coffee beans
1 tsp pepper
½ tsp finely ground cardamom
1 frying chicken cut into serving size pieces
Zest of one lemon

Mix coffee, pepper, and cardamom, together. Dust onto chicken pieces. Let stand for one hour. Preheat oven to 375 and bake until tender about 30 minutes.
Sprinkle with lemon zest Will make 4 servings

Brenda Stockdale (my sister) Kitchener, Ontario, Canada

From my great niece (nice!) 9 years of age (unedited)

Ice Cream Parlour Mocha Sodas   Serves 4 Ingredients:

½ cup half water
4 scoops or chocolate ice
8 tea spoons finely ground coffee
1 quart club soda
2 cups milk
sweetened whipped cream

Place hot water in a medium sized pitcher. Stir in coffee. Finely grind into a powder texture, dissolved. Stir in milk. Place one scoop of ice cream into each of 4 ice cream soda glasses. Coffee/milk mixture equally into each glass. Fill glasses almost to brim with club soda top sweetened whipping cream.

your great nice, Kierstin Munce. Waterloo Ontario Canada.

Thanks to my family for simply being there.

It was predestined to happen…

From that very first fateful sip, I knew it was going to be a lifetime love affair. When we were kids, my parents would keep their leftover coffee in a container in the refrigerator. Whenever my sisters and I craved a sweet treat, we would combine the coffee with a *lot* of cream and a *lot* of sugar. When I was a baby, my Dad's mother, my Nana (born in Belfast, Ireland, wouldn't enter a church without a hat and gloves, heaven forbid if a lady ever wore trousers) would give me a tablespoon of half coffee and half milk. She created in me a passion that lives to this day.

Black coffee, in its purest form, contains many cup characteristics. It has many tones and nuances. Brew a pot. Pour a cup. Let it sit for awhile, just to cool down a little. Take a sip. Swirl it in your mouth, just to aerate it. Concentrate on what are the higher and lower notes. There is a term they use in the coffee industry called 'mouth feel.' It describes the feeling on your tongue. Some coffees 'feel' heavy. Some 'feel' light. Two words that describe coffee are body and acidity. The body is the feel on your tongue. Acidity is the higher note in your cup--not a bad thing! Envision milk and orange juice. Milk, which is heavy, represents the body. Orange juice, with its bright edge, represents the acidity. Do you get the idea? Every coffee producing country yields its own cup characteristics.

Many African coffees are reputed to have a winey taste. Indonesians are famous for their deep, complex, earthy tones. Many South American coffees are said to be brighter in the cup due to their acidity. For fans of a milder, well balanced cup, Jamaica and Hawaii produce awesome coffees. Coffee is like wine. As I mentioned before, every country, every region, produces its own unique brew. Many variables factor into the end product--from elevation, to rainfall, to sunlight, to shade, to volcanic soil. Very labor intensive . . . but well worth the effort.

Coffee, in its purest form, is an indulgence. To fully comprehend all of its nuances, you have to acquire a taste to enjoy it black--no cream, no sugar. However, coffee is very versatile. It lends itself and its complexity to many avenues in your kitchen. Just for an example, to touch the tip of the iceberg, liven up your favorite brew with some of these:

- Flavoring syrups. The most popular are vanilla, caramel, almond and hazelnut. They both flavor and sweeten. There are many, many flavors from which to choose. Visit Monin.com for a treasure trove of flavors.
- Chocolate syrup. Coffee 'marries' with chocolate. They are the perfect pair. I have to use this word again--complexity. It is the ultimate union. Choose a quality brand of chocolate. For a taste of Americana, you can't beat Hershey's chocolate. They have been producing quality chocolate syrup for home use since 1928. Visit the American icon at Hersheys.com
- Whipped cream. Pass by that tub or aerosol can of whipped cream in the supermarket. Make your own! Utilizing a commercial cream whipper opens the door to many possibilities. I recommend a company by the name of isi- they make both the cream whipper and the cream chargers required to make your own whipped cream. Use heavy cream or liquid whipping cream. It

is as easy as filling the whipper with cream, screwing on the lid and inserting the cream charger. Homemade whipped cream! Be creative--try making flavored whipped cream by adding a shot of flavoring syrup or chocolate. My favorite flavored whipped cream is chocolate caramel. Visit isinorthamerica.com for more information.

Toppings

Home made whipped cream . . . of course!
Frothed milk . . . oh, yeah.
Ice cream? Uh huh.
Crushed nuts
Vanilla sugar
Candy sprinkles
shaved chocolate
chocolate sugar
heavy or regular flavoring syrup
Grated orange/lemon peel
Coconut (regular or toasted)
Ground cinnamon
Ground chocolate
Fresh or candied fruit
Crushed cookies
Crumbled candy bars

– Can you think of more? --

You can add

Whole milk
Flavoring syrups
Honey
2% milk
White sugar
Heavy syrups- chocolate, caramel, strawberry
Skim milk

Brown sugar
Half & half cream
Molasses
Non-alcohol based extracts
Spirits or liqueurs
Soy milk
Dark brown sugar
Rice milk

Perfect accompaniments

Biscotti
Cookie spoons
Piroulines
fresh fruit
Rock candy swizzle sticks
Wafer cookies
Candy sticks
Cinnamon sticks
hard candy
Nuts
Chocolate spoons
Chocolate covered espresso beans

Tip! Make your own chocolate sugar by combining cocoa powder and granulated sugar. Make cinnamon sugar with granulated sugar mixed with ground cinnamon.

To make vanilla sugar, scrape the seeds from one vanilla bean into 2 cups of granulated sugar. Stir to combine. Insert the scraped vanilla bean into the mix and cover tightly in an airtight container. Let sit in a dark cabinet for two weeks. Remove the bean before using. You can add more sugar as you use your supply, simply shake it in. You will know when you need to make more by the weakening vanilla flavor.

The recipes

Hot Regular Brewed Coffee Drinks

Cold Regular Brewed Coffee Drinks

Hot Espresso Based Coffee Drinks

Cold Espresso Based Coffee Drinks

Utilizing Coffee in Entrees

Utilizing Coffee in Desserts

Hot Regular Brewed Coffee Drinks

When making all coffee based drinks, remember this: Presentation is important. Find different ceramic bowls with matching or un-matching saucers. Glassware is great because it allows you to view the brew and its toppings. Visualize. Remember we eat "and drink" with our eyes. Your drinks can look and taste great too! I am going to begin each chapter in the recipe portion of Celebrating the Bean with one or two of my own creations. Try these . . .

My Nutty Buddy

1 six ounce cup regular brewed coffee
1 ounce each hazelnut and praline flavored syrups
Half and half cream to your color preference
Almond and chocolate flavored whipped cream
2 Pirouline cookies
Hazelnuts and Pecans

Flavor the liquid whipping cream with 3 ounces heavy chocolate syrup and 3 ounces almond flavored syrup. Put on the lid and charge. Add hazelnut/praline syrups to brewed coffee along with half and half cream. Top with whipped cream. Serve the cup on a saucer. Insert piroulines into the whipped cream and garnish the saucer with the hazelnuts and pecans. Nuts to you.

Roasted Caramel Chocolat

1six ounce cup French roast coffee
1 ounce heavy chocolate syrup, 1 ounce regular caramel syrup
Steamed milk
Caramels
Regular whipped cream, wafer cookie
Heavy chocolate and heavy caramel syrup, as well as unsweetened cocoa powder to garnish

A chocolate colored cup; a caramel colored saucer. Pour coffee into a cup and flavor with chocolate and caramel syrups. Top with whipped cream then drizzle cream with chocolate and caramel syrup. Sprinkle with unsweetened cocoa powder. Wedge the wafer cookie into the cream. Lay a few chocolate and caramel caramels on the saucer. Yummm!

Tip . . .purchase a squeezable plastic dispenser to drizzle your heavy syrups; you can warm it on low heat in your microwave to make it easier to "drizzle."

Syrups...whether heavy, such as chocolate , strawberry, and

caramel, or light, such as those sold specifically to flavor specialty drinks(water based) add a great range to your options when making coffee based drinks. Both can be used to both flavor as well as garnish, although heavy syrups are the king when drizzled on top of whipped cream for presentation. Heavy syrups are also sold specifically as ice cream toppings – these can easily be substituted as a drizzle. The following is a list of only a few flavoring syrups available, and some great combinations to liven up your regular coffee.

Almond	Irish Cream
Anise	Lemon
Apple	Lime
Banana	Pecan (praline)
Blackberry	Macadamia Nut
Blueberry	Maple
Butterscotch	Marshmallow
Caramel	Orange
Cherry	Peppermint
Chocolate- Dark, Mint, White	Pineapple
Cinnamon	Pistachio
Coconut	Raspberry
Coffee	Rum
Crème de Cacoa	Strawberry
Ginger	Toffee
Hazelnut	Vanilla

Try any of these combinations…

Almond Joy- almond, chocolate, coconut

Caramellow- caramel, vanilla, marshmallow

Cinnamon Pecan- cinnamon, praline

Black Forest Cake- dark chocolate, cherry, vanilla

German Chocolate Cake- crème de cacao, white chocolate, coconut

Hawaiian – macadamia nut, banana, pineapple

Rum Ball- dark chocolate, rum, coconut

Spiced Nuts- hazelnut, pistachio, cinnamon

Toffee Coffee- caramel, toffee

Tuity Fruity- 3 of your favorite fruit flavored syrups

Vanilla Nut- vanilla, your favorite nut flavored syrup

White Chocolate Mocha- dark chocolate, white chocolate

Tip- the kids, with their insatiable sweet tooth's, will find many ways to use your syrups. For example, try them over ice cream. Old time fountain drinks were flavored with flavored syrups. Many coffee houses and ice cream parlors still use syrups to create a delicious cold drink- the Italian Soda. Italian sodas utilize mostly the fruit flavored syrups; however any syrup can be used. Try a soda with coffee syrup for a more grown up taste. To make Italian sodas, simply fill a glass half full with ice, add soda water, and flavor with syrup. Top your soda with whipped cream and a straw and you are ready to not only quench your thirst, but indulge in a treat. For an even more indulgent treat, rather than whipped cream, float heavy cream on top of your drink. Mmmmm...

Recipes I have gathered over the years, for anytime you or your company crave a regular coffee treat-

Café Liegeois

1 scoop vanilla ice cream
½ c. dark hot coffee
Honey flavored syrup sweetened whipped cream
Grated milk chocolate
Pour coffee into a large mug and add the ice cream. Top with cream and grated chocolate. Serves 1

Chocolate Citrus

6 ounces hot full city roast coffee
2 squares Ghirardelli chocolate
Juice of ½ of an orange
Chocolate and orange infused whipped cream

Put several squares of chocolate into a large cup. (Ghirardelli dark chocolate is awesome!) Pour dark roast coffee over top. Stir well to melt chocolate. Add the juice from half an orange. Top with whipped cream and indulge yourself. Serves 1

Traditional Viennese Coffee

This wonderful blend of coffee, cream, and chocolate is rich and decadent.

2 tablespoons heavy cream
2 ounces chopped semisweet chocolate
2 cups dark roast coffee
Whipped cream
Cinnamon

Put the cream and chocolate in a saucepan. Place over low heat and cook, stirring frequently, until the chocolate is melted and smooth. Slowly whisk in the hot coffee. Pour into cups and top with whipped cream and cinnamon.
Serves 2

Borgian Coffee

6 oz. Dark roast coffee
6 oz. Dark hot chocolate
Whipped cream
Grated orange peel

Combine brewed coffee and hot chocolate in cup. Top with whipped cream. Sprinkle grated orange peel on top
Serves 2

European Blend

(A wee bit of elegance)

1 ½ cups strong coffee
1 egg white
¼ teaspoon vanilla extract
2 tablespoons half and half

Beat egg white until it forms soft peaks Add vanilla and continue to beat until stiff peaks are formed. Spoon into 2 coffee mugs. Pour coffee over egg white and top with half and half. Serves 2

Chocolate Cream

4 teaspoons chocolate syrup
½ cup heavy cream
¾ teaspoon cinnamon
¼ teaspoon nutmeg
1 tablespoon sugar
1-½ cups extra-strength hot coffee

Put 1 teaspoon chocolate syrup into each of 4 small cups. In a blender, combine cream, cinnamon, nutmeg and sugar. Blend until creamy, not whipped. Pour coffee into cups. Stir to blend with syrup. Top with whipped cream. Serves 4

Black Forest Coffee

4 cups hot brewed coffee
½ cup chocolate syrup
¼ cup maraschino cherry juice
Whipped cream
Chocolate syrup
Maraschino cherry

Combine hot coffee, chocolate syrup, and maraschino cherry juice; mix well. Pour into mugs. Top with whipped cream and a cherry, and drizzle with chocolate syrup.. Serves 4

Mochalatte
(I like it a lot!)

2 cups strong coffee
⅓ cup cocoa powder
2 cups milk
4 tbsps sugar
½ teaspoon vanilla extract
½ cup whipping cream
dash cinnamon

Mix cocoa, sugar, coffee and milk in a sauce pan Heat, over medium heat constantly stirring, until simmering. Remove from heat and stir in vanilla. Pour into cups, top with whipped cream and cinnamon. Serves 4

Mexican Coffee

¾ cup coffee beans, ground
2 teaspoons ground cinnamon
6 cups water
1 cup milk
⅓ cup chocolate syrup
2 tablespoons light brown sugar
1 teaspoon pure vanilla extract
whipped cream & ground cinnamon

Place coffee and cinnamon in filter basket of coffee maker and brew. In a saucepan, blend milk, chocolate syrup and sugar. Stir over low heat until sugar dissolves. When hot and simmering, add brewed coffee to milk mixture. Stir in vanilla. Pour into cups and garnish with whipped cream and cinnamon. Serves 6

...using regular brewed coffee and any combination of flavoring syrups, milk, cream, or rice/soy milk, whipped cream and toppings, experiment....

Poor Man's Café Mocha (or starving students)

One 8 oz cup Robusta coffee,
One envelope of instant hot chocolate mix.

Rip off the top of the envelope of instant hot chocolate mix. Pour contents of envelope into a Styrofoam cup. Add

8 oz of Robusta coffee. Stir mixture as briskly as possible with a re-usable plastic spoon to obtain cream like froth. Enjoy.

North of the border

My parents are Canadian. I was born in the United States, however my parents moved me to Canada when I was 7 years old. We moved from Boston, Massachusetts to a rural dairy farm in the province of Ontario. Canadian Culture Shock! I knew I liked coffee with my milk; I just didn't understand where milk came from. I found out quickly. Don't get me wrong, not all of Canada is rural. The country also has many diverse large cities, and their own diverse love of coffee. Their love of coffee is named after a hockey player. (You aren't allowed to be a Canadian if you aren't a hockey fan). This is my tribute to my family and all fine Canadians north of the border.

Canadian Coffee

Get out of bed, get ready. Get into your car. Drive to Tim Horton's. Go in, wait in line. Purchase a large cup: cream and sugar is optional. Buy a walnut crunch for the side. Get back into your car. If you are working, drink coffee on the way, if not, sip slowly and finish at home. (This recipe can be increased quite easily if you have houseguests or fellow passengers.)

After Dinner Delights

Cafe Canadienne

Now this is the real Canadian version of coffee.

¼ cup plus 4 teaspoons real Canadian maple syrup
¾ cup Canadian Rye whiskey
3 cups of double strength coffee
1 cup whipping cream

Whip cream flavored with 4 teaspoons of maple syrup until it makes soft peaks Divide whiskey and maple syrup equally into 4 cups. Pour hot coffee into cups, leaving room for whipped cream. Serves 4

Quick and easy Grasshopper

To one cup freshly brewed coffee add 1 ounce Chocolate Mint Liqueur. Top with whipped cream and shaved chocolate. Quick. Easy. Serves 1

Café Royale

Place a sugar cube on a spoon over a cup of hot black coffee. Pour an ounce of bourbon through the lump (which in turn runs into the coffee). Light the soaked sugar cube and let it burn out. Add the cube to the coffee and stir. Serves 1

Liqueur Au Lait

1 ½ tbsp. of your favorite liqueur
½ c. strong hot coffee
½ c. hot milk

Pour liqueur into a tall mug. Fill with coffee and milk. Serves 1

Italian Coffee

4 ounces freshly brewed
Italian roast coffee
1 tablespoon Amaretto liqueur
1 tablespoon brandy
¼ cup heavy cream, warmed
¼ teaspoon cinnamon

Pour coffee into a tempered glass cup. Sweeten, if desired. Add the almond liqueur and brandy and stir. Pour the cream slowly and carefully over the back of a teaspoon so that it floats on top of the drink. Dust with cinnamon. Serves 1

Jamaican Me Crazy
(You really are)

2 cups strong coffee
2 oz. Kahlua
2 oz. dark rum

whipped cream
2 dashes of nutmeg
Mix the Kahlua and rum, pour into 2 cups
Add coffee and stir
Top with whipped cream and a dash of nutmeg
Serves 2

Kahlua Mocha

1.5 oz Kahlua liqueur
4 oz plain chocolate
1 cup hot black coffee
 thickened lightly whipped cream
Chocolate covered espresso beans

Slowly melt chocolate in a low to medium heat saucepan being careful not to burn it. Gradually add the coffee and liqueur as you gently heat. Pour the liquid into two warmed brandy balloons and spoon the cream on top. Garnish with chocolate covered espresso beans. Serves 2

Eggnog Caffe

2 cups eggnog
2 tbsp rum
1 tbsp bourbon
1 cup hot brewed coffee

Put eggnog in a small pan over medium heat. When hot, add brewed coffee and Spirits. Whisk until frothy. Serves 2

Southern Sensation

(An after dinner decadence)

4 cups dark roast coffee
½ cup Kahlua liqueur
4 tablespoons Southern Comfort liqueur
Sugar to taste
whipping cream
Grated semisweet chocolate

Combine coffee, Kahlua and Southern Comfort. Add sugar to taste. Divide equally between 4 cups. Whisk cream in a saucepan over medium heat until hot and frothy, about 2-3 minutes. Spoon hot cream over coffee. Top cream with grated chocolate. Serves 4

Tia Maria Candida

3-1 oz. bitter chocolate squares
⅓ cup sugar
6 cups milk
1 t. vanilla
½ cup Tia Maria coffee liqueur

Over low heat melt the chocolate squares until they soften.

Add the milk and sugar. Whisk until combined. Remove from heat and stir in vanilla and Tia Maria. Pour into mugs and serve immediately. Serves 4 - 6

Chocolate Brandy for a Crowd

8 cups hot brewed coffee
8 ounces coffee flavored liqueur
8 ounces brandy
4 ounces crème de cacao
2 cups whipped cream to garnish
Chocolate sprinkles

In the bottom of 8 coffee mugs, pour 1 ounce each coffee liqueur and brandy. Pour in ½ ounce each crème de cacao. Fill each cup with hot coffee and garnish with a dollop of whipped cream and chocolate sprinkles. Serves 6 - 8

It's really getting hot in here. Gotta cool things down a bit.

Cold Regular Brewed Coffee Drinks

Anybody who has ever ordered a cup of regular coffee in a restaurant or coffee house has heard these words: "May I warm that up for you?" If you want it hot, yes is the definitive answer. However, if you want it cold, right then and there, here and now, you are definitely in the right place! If you are a fan of any iced coffee beverage, you have to purchase a Toddy coffee maker. It's a product many purveyors of cold coffee drinks would rather keep a secret. To make your own Toddy iced coffee at home, try this . . .

Using regular coffee, follow the directions to make the Toddy concentrate found in the brewer section of the book. With a combination of ⅓ concentrate to ⅔ milk (or half and half cream if you want a breve), make the base for your iced drink. Now, sweeten and flavor your brew with flavoring syrup. Try a simple vanilla mixture to start with. Notice how smooth and rich it is; although you are flavoring it, the coffee's essence is still very evident. There are many coffee houses which still use this method for their own signature drinks. Taking into account how many flavoring syrups are available, can you imagine all the recipes you will be creating in the very near future?

Try buying a pound of coffee that has already been flavored. I would suggest having the shop grind it for you so as not to introduce any unwanted flavor into your home grinder. Many coffee shops that sell whole bean have two separate grinders for regular and flavored coffee. The nice thing about going in this direction is that you can use a sugar substitute if you have to stay away from regular sugar. From the bottom of my heart, a very warm thank you for your cold coffee concentrate, Mr. Todd Simpson.

These are a few of my own toddy iced coffee creations made with regular coffee...

V.L.T. (Vanilla Layered Toddy)

16 oz cup
⅓ Toddy concentrate
⅓ whole milk
⅓ half & half cream
3 oz vanilla syrup
Vanilla infused whipped cream

Always begin your cold Toddy by filling a glass half full of ice. Add the concentrate to ⅓ full. Now add milk, ½ and ½ cream, and vanilla syrup. Stir. Top with vanilla whipped cream. If I serve this to guests, I garnish the saucer with a few vanilla flavored cookies and a vanilla chocolate spoon. It's vanillalicious!

Cinnamon Almond Swirl

16 oz cup
⅓ Concentrate, ⅔ whole milk
Equal parts almond and cinnamon syrups (1 ½ oz each)
Whipped cream

Top flavored Toddy mixture with whipped cream and finish with sweet sugar cinnamon and crushed almonds. Garnish with a cinnamon stick to swirl.

Keepin' it cool...

Coffee Iced Cubes, traditional iced coffee
Brew regular coffee, let it cool and pour into ice cube trays. Freeze. Make coffee just the way you like it, chill it, and then pour it over the coffee cubes. This keeps the coffee strong even as the ice melts.

Another useful tip to flavor any iced coffee? Granulated sugar is difficult to incorporate into cold liquids. Use the following recipe for simple sugar syrup to sweeten all of your cold drinks.

Simple syrup

4 cups Water
1 pound Sugar

Dissolve sugar in water and bring to a low boil. Be careful to stir constantly so as not to let the mixture boil over. When the sugar has completely dissolved, remove from heat and cool before using. Keep refrigerated up to 3 weeks. Makes 7 cups

Coffee Banana Shake

1 ½ cups coffee, chilled
6 tbsp. sugar (or simple sugar to taste)
2 ripe bananas
2 cups vanilla ice cream

Cut bananas into chunks and mix with coffee and sugar. Blend at high speed until smooth. Add ice cream and blend on medium until smooth. Serves 2

Fruity Coffee Shake

¾ cups dark roast coffee, chilled
½ cup frozen blueberries
½ cup half & half cream
2 cups vanilla ice cream
2 tsp vanilla extract
2 tbsp chocolate syrup

Combine all ingredients in a blender. Blend until completely smooth. Substitute any frozen fruit for a different twist. Serves 2

Chocolate Strawberry Frappe

1 ½ cups strawberry ice cream
¼ cup chocolate syrup
3 tablespoons sugar (or simple syrup)
1 cup strong, brewed coffee, chilled
1 cup ice cubes
Whipped cream

Combine the ice cream, chocolate syrup and sugar in your blender. Pulse until just blended. Add the coffee and ice cubes and blend at high speed until fully blended. Pour into glasses. Top with a dollop of whipped cream and garnish with fresh strawberry slices. Serves 2

French Roast Chiller
(One of my favorites)

¾ cup French(or darker) roast coffee chilled
2 scoops vanilla ice cream
½ cup whole milk
2 tbsp sugar(optional)

Place the coffee in a blender. Add the ice cream, sugar, and milk. Blend. Great for the not so sweet coffee fan. Serves 2

Chocolate Cinnamon Shake

1 cup brewed coffee at room temperature
1 cup chocolate ice cream
1 cup milk
1 cup crushed ice
1½ teaspoons ground cinnamon
Combine all in blender and blend until smooth. Serves 2

Mocha Smoothie.

⅓ cup milk
⅔ cup chilled black, sweetened coffee
3 scoops coffee ice cream
3 scoops chocolate ice cream

Combine all the Ingredients in a blender until creamy. Pour into tall glasses and enjoy. Serves 2

Slushy Cooler

1 ½ c. cold coffee
1 ½ c. chocolate ice cream
¼ c. heavy chocolate syrup
Crushed ice
Whipped cream

In a blender place coffee, ice cream and syrup. Cover; blend until smooth. Serve immediately over crushed ice. Top with whipped cream. Serves 2

Coffee Fizz

2 ½ cups dark roast coffee
2 teaspoons sugar
⅔ cup half and half cream
4 scoops of coffee flavored ice cream
1 large bottle of your favorite cola

Sweeten hot coffee with sugar and chill. Mix coffee with half and half cream. Fill 4 tall glasses half full of coffee/cream mixture. Add one scoop of ice cream to each glass. Top with cola. FIZZZZZ. Serves 4

French Coffee Granita

3 cups cold French roast coffee
1 ½ cups sugar
1 pint whipping cream
1 quart whole milk
2 tsp. vanilla

Mix together and freeze. Take out 1 hour before serving Scrape with a fork until slushy. Serves 4- 6

….regular iced coffee is as easy as having room temperature coffee on hand, poured over coffee ice cubes. Doctor it up any way you like it….

After dinner treats for the older crowd

Brandy Freeze

1 cup dark roast coffee, chilled
2 tablespoons sugar
1 cup half and half
3 oz brandy
6 ice cubes
whipped cream

Place all ingredients into blender. Mix until ice is blended Pour into tall glasses and top with whipped cream. Serves 2

Iced Bourbon Breve

2 cups dark roast coffee, cooled
2 tbsp. brown sugar
3 tbsp. heavy chocolate syrup
2 cups half-and-half cream
3 oz. bourbon whiskey (substitute your favorite spirit)

Dissolve sugar and chocolate syrup in hot coffee. Let cool. Add half-and-half and bourbon. Chill and serve over ice. Serves 2

Amaretto Granita

1 cup water
½ cup sugar
3 cups French roast coffee
⅓ cup amaretto liqueur
½ & ½ cream

Combine water and sugar in a small saucepan. Place on a burner over medium high heat until it comes to a boil. Cook just until sugar dissolves. Remove from heat; stir in the coffee and the amaretto. Pour into a 13 x 9 inch baking dish and let cool. Cover; freeze at least 4 hours. Remove mixture from freezer. Using a fork, scrape the coffee ice. Serve coffee granita in decorative wine glasses with a splash of ½ & ½ cream. Serves 2

Irish Mocha Frappe

1 cup dark roast coffee
2 cups milk
8 teaspoons cocoa powder
2 cups Baileys Irish Cream liqueur

In a small saucepan, combine coffee, milk and cocoa.
Heat the mixture over moderate heat, whisking, until the cocoa is dissolved, and let it cool. Stir in ½ cup of the Baileys. Pour the mixture into ice cube trays and freeze. Place ice cubes in blender with remaining Baileys. Blend until smooth, but still frozen Serves 2

Creamy Café Frangelico

2 cups chilled strong coffee
⅔ cup sweetened condensed milk
⅔ cup half & half cream
Café frangelico liqueur

Combine coffee and condensed milk. Whisk in half & half cream until blended. Pour over ice in a tall glass and add liqueur to your taste. Serves 2

Iced Spiced Coffee

2 cups of strong coffee, cold
4 oz. light rum
3 tablespoons sugar
2 tablespoons light cream
2 cinnamon sticks
pinch of powdered cloves
pinch of allspice

Whisk all ingredients, pour over ice, and serve with cinnamon sticks to stir. Serves 2

Amaretto Iced Coffee

3 cups coffee, cold
2 cups vanilla ice cream
1 cup milk
¼ cup amaretto liqueur
2 tsp vanilla extract
1 tsp almond extract
Crushed ice

Combine everything except ice in a blender and whip until smooth. Fill glasses half full with crushed ice, and fill the rest with coffee mixture. Serves 4- 6

Frozen Coffee Cooler

6 C. ice cubes
4 C. brewed coffee, cooled
1 C. coffee liqueur
¾ C. sugar
1 t. ground cinnamon
1 C. half & half cream
whipped cream, ground cinnamon

Process half of first 5 ingredients in a blender until smooth. Pour coffee mixture into a large pitcher. Repeat with remaining half of first 5 ingredients, and add to the pitcher. Stir half-and-half into coffee mixture. Serve immediately. Serves 4- 6

Iced Delite

8 cups brewed coffee, cooled
1 cup milk
1 cup half-and-half cream
⅓ cup white sugar
2 teaspoons vanilla extract
8 tablespoons crème de cacao

In a pitcher, combine cooled coffee, milk and half-and-half. Stir in sugar, vanilla and crème de cacao. Chill in refrigerator until ready to serve. Serves 4- 6

Enough of the regular brewed coffee drinks already. Let's get onboard the Espresso Express!

Hot Espresso Coffee Based Drinks

In my mind, the most awesome aspect of being a coffee fan is the ability to take the traditional espresso based specialty coffee drinks and pull them out of their comfort zones. Lately, even though I don't eat much fruit, I've been on a fruit and dark chocolate craze with my coffee. These are two goodies I put together one rainy Florida afternoon.

Dark Chocolate Cherry Bomb

I call this drink a cherry bomb because you "drop" a dark chocolate and espresso infused bomb into the cherry steamed milk. It looks great in a glass cup. Steam and froth milk which has had two shots of cherry flavored syrup stirred into it. It becomes very pink. Set milk aside and pull a double shot of espresso. Put two shots of heavy dark chocolate syrup into the espresso and swirl to combine the two. (Melt some Ghirardelli dark chocolate squares) Now, pour the steamed, frothed milk into the glass cup. Finally, drop the bomb! Pour the espresso and chocolate mixture directly into the center of the frothed milk. Top with chocolate sugar and garnish the finished drink with two cherries on the stem.

Mandarin Orange Mocha

A taste of Southeast Asia is what I strived for, from the peak of the whipped cream to the bottom of the cup.

Steam milk blended with 2 shots of mandarin syrup. Set aside and pull a double espresso. Add 2 shots heavy dark chocolate syrup to the espresso and swirl to mix. Pour the flavored milk into your cup. Now pour the espresso/chocolate mixture into the steamed milk. Top with whipped cream. (Flavor the cream with equal amounts of mandarin and vanilla flavoring syrup.) Garnish the saucer with Ghirardelli dark chocolate squares and segments of fresh mandarin oranges.

....I always pour my espresso into the steamed milk-rather than the milk into the espresso. I feel that if you don't preheat your cups your espresso shot will be cooled upon contact-it also makes for better presentation if you are serving guests.

TIP: Buy shot glasses to brew your espresso coffee into. Shot glasses are measured in increments of ounces, enabling you to achieve the perfect short or long espresso shot. To ensure a proper 1 ½ oz. shot of flavoring syrup, posi pours are available. They fit into the top of the flavoring syrup bottle. Any fine kitchenware store will carry posi pours.

Alright, everybody, lets get on board!
The Espresso Express

While onboard, don't forget the younger crowd! They need to be involved as well. Only one word will suffice, steamer. A steamer is simply milk combined with flavoring syrup that is steamed. No coffee is required. The youngsters will love to partake in steaming, dreaming up recipes and flavoring their own whipped cream. Celebrate the Bean, kid style. (Adult supervision is absolutely mandatory in this venture.)

All of the following hot espresso based recipes are my own creations. It certainly isn't difficult to customize your own signature drinks. What are the ingredients in your favorite chocolate bar? How about your favorite dessert? Using combinations of syrups, chocolates, and garnishes, create your own repertoire. All of my recipes are made to serve one, but can be increased.

Gingerbread Con Panna

Single shot espresso
1 oz gingerbread flavored syrup
1 oz vanilla syrup
6 ounces milk, steamed
Whipped cream
nutmeg
cinnamon sugars

Combine espresso coffee with flavored syrups. Add steamed milk to your favorite coffee cup. Pour espresso into steamed milk. Top with whipped cream, and sprinkle with nutmeg and cinnamon sugar.

Pumpkin Breve

A taste of autumn, all year long.

Single shot espresso
6 ounces ½ & ½ cream
1 ½oz cinnamon syrup
1 tbsp (or to taste) pureed canned pumpkin
Sweet nutmeg sugar.

Spoon pumpkin into the bottom of your cup. Lightly froth ½ & ½ cream. Brew a single espresso and add cinnamon syrup to it. Pour steamed ½ & ½ into your cup and stir to mix with canned pumpkin. Pour the espresso into the pumpkin mixture and top with nutmeg sugar.

Turtle Soy Sundae

(Substitute soymilk, all of you health nuts)

Single shot espresso
6 oz soy milk
¾ oz chocolate syrup (or carob syrup)
⅓ oz each caramel and praline syrup
Very little, or no whipped cream

Steam soy milk and pour into an environmentally friendly cup. Add carob syrup to soy and stir. Pull an espresso and add caramel and praline syrup to it. Pour into soy mixture. (whipped cream is definitely optional)

Coconut Cream Latte

Single shot espresso
6 oz whole milk
¾ oz. coconut syrup
¼ oz. Irish cream syrup.
Shredded toasted coconut

Steam and lightly froth whole milk. Add syrups to espresso. Pour lightly frothed milk into your cup, add flavored espresso. Sprinkle with shredded toasted coconut

Raspberry Almond Mocha

Single shot espresso
6 oz whole milk
½ oz. thick chocolate syrup
¼ oz. each raspberry and almond syrups
Whipped cream

Add raspberry and almond syrups to milk and steam. Pull espresso shot, stir in chocolate syrup and add to mix. Top with whipped cream. Drizzle some extra raspberry and almond syrup on the whipped cream.

Nutty Irish Cappuccino

Single shot espresso
6 oz whole milk
¾ oz. each Irish cream and hazelnut syrups
Finely crushed hazelnuts to garnish

Add Irish cream and hazelnut syrups to milk and froth. Set flavored, frothed mixture aside. Pull a shot of espresso. Pour frothed milk into a cup. Pour espresso shot through froth into the steamed milk Sprinkle finely crushed hazelnuts on top.

Butterscotch Meltdown

Single shot espresso
3 oz whole milk
3 oz ½ &½ cream
1 oz. butterscotch syrup, ½ oz caramel syrup
Whipped cream
Heavy caramel syrup to garnish

Add butterscotch syrup and caramel syrup to milk and ½ & ½ mixture. Steam and set aside. Pull a shot of espresso. Pour flavored milk into a cup. Pour espresso shot into the steamed milk Top with whipped cream and drizzle with heavy caramel syrup and extra butterscotch syrup.

Cinnamon Pecan Breve

Single shot espresso
6 oz ½ & ½ cream
1 oz. pecan (praline) syrup, 1oz cinnamon syrup
Cinnamon sugar to garnish

Add cinnamon syrup and pecan syrup to ½ & ½ cream. Steam to get a light froth and set aside. Pull a shot of espresso. Pour flavored cream into a cup. Pour espresso shot through froth into the steamed milk Dust with cinnamon sugar.

Peanut Butter Mocha

(Makes a bowlful)

Double shot espresso
12 oz whole milk
2 oz heavy chocolate syrup
2 tbsp smooth peanut butter
Whipped cream
Crushed peanuts

Steam milk. Add peanut butter to milk and stir until blended. Meanwhile, pull a double espresso. Add heavy chocolate syrup to espresso and combine. Pour peanut butter milk into a large cup and saucer. Add espresso and chocolate. Stir. Top with whipped cream and crushed peanuts. Sweet tooth? Drizzle heavy chocolate syrup on top as well.

Hazelnut Mocha

(Makes a bowlful)

Double shot espresso
12 oz whole milk
½ oz heavy chocolate syrup
1 oz hazelnut syrup
2 tbsp hazelnut spread (such as Nutella)
Whipped cream
Crushed hazelnuts

Steam milk. Add hazelnut spread plus 1 oz hazelnut syrup to milk. Stir until blended. Meanwhile, pull a double espresso. Add heavy chocolate syrup to espresso and combine. Pour hazelnut milk into a large cup and saucer. Add espresso and chocolate. Top with whipped cream and crushed hazelnuts.

From hot coffee to cold, it just never gets old...

Cold Espresso Coffee Based Drinks

Back to my beloved Toddy. Use coarsely ground espresso roast coffee and take your concentrate to new heights. An iced latte is as simple as concentrate and milk. To make an iced mocha, make chocolate milk (ya gotta use Hershey's chocolate!), mix with concentrate and top with whipped cream. Earlier I mentioned the concentrate's versatility. It now comes to the forefront. This is a recipe I serve at Christmas. Cold coffee at Christmas, you might ask? Oh, yeah. I moved to the south many years ago and now enjoy Christmas day on my patio with friends, basking in the sun. It's kind of a tradition. Gather your family and friends on Christmas day, celebrate the birth, celebrate the bean, simply celebrate.

Christmas Toddy

O.K., O.K I know the measurement of concentrate to milk is ⅓ to ⅔rds, however, it's Christmas. I can't deal with the math--it was my worst subject in school. I just rounded the numbers up.

2 ½ cups espresso based toddy concentrate
5 ½ cups whole milk
8 shots heavy chocolate syrup
4 shots peppermint syrup
Whipped cream to top
Red and green candy sprinkles
Candy cane

Combine all liquid ingredients in a large pitcher and stir to mix. Pour into 4 glasses half filled with ice. Top with whipped cream and candy sprinkles. Poke the candy cane into the whipped cream at any angle you prefer.

Anytime you want to make a traditional iced cappuccino, latte, or mocha, always put the ice in your cup first, followed by the milk, followed by your espresso shot, to ensure that your espresso shot does not get diluted.

Traditional Iced Cafe Latte

Add ice to your glass, then pour in the milk until glass is ¾ full. Pour a double shot of espresso into the milk and ice mixture. Stir.

Traditional Iced Cappuccino

Froth milk quickly to obtain froth, keeping milk relatively cool. Pour milk and froth over ice. If you want your drink flavored, pour syrup into your espresso shot. Pour flavored espresso shot into the ice and milk froth mixture.

Traditional Iced Café Mocha

Pour milk into a cup of ice up to ¾ full. Pull a double espresso and swirl two shots of heavy chocolate syrup into it. Pour into milk and stir. Top with whipped cream.

My Couch Potato Iced Banana Split

Put down the remote, get off your couch and go to the kitchen. Get a banana. Split it. (Just cut it in half--lengthways, mind you.) Put some ice in a large cup and pour in some vanilla flavored milk (or half & half cream, if you're feeling like a breve). Pull a double shot of espresso. Add two shots of banana flavored syrup to the espresso and pour into the milk. Stir and top with whipped cream. Drizzle heavy caramel, strawberry, and chocolate syrup on top of the whipped cream. Top with crushed nuts and (of course!) a cherry. Insert half of the banana into the whipped cream and wrap the other half around the saucer. Grab a straw and go bananas!

Iced Espresso Fizz

(A more serious beverage)

Fill a 16 ounce cup to ¾ full with ice and soda water
Add a double espresso
Add 1 ½ oz. of flavoring syrup.
Stir with a straw and enjoy
Flavor your fizz with any of your favorite syrups.
Serves 1

Espresso, Shaken, Not Stirred

(Are you really serious? Yes, Mr. Bond.)

Triple shot espresso, freshly pulled
Ice cubes
1 ½ oz vanilla syrup
a twist of lemon peel

Fill a cocktail shaker halfway with ice cubes. Add vanilla syrup. Pour the espresso over the ice and shake vigorously for 10 to15 seconds. Strain into a martini glass.
Twist the lemon peel zest into the mix.
Serves 1

Nonfat Yogurt Espresso Smoothie

Triple espresso, cooled
1 cup non-fat frozen yogurt
½ cup ice cubes
1 ½ tbsp sugar
Combine and blend until smooth
Serves 1

Easy Iced Vietnamese Coffee

Double shot espresso
8 oz sweetened condensed milk
Ice
Fill a tall glass with ice. Add sweetened condensed milk. Pour in your espresso shot. Stir, sip and enjoy. Serves 1

Homemade Frappuccino

2 double espressos, cooled
2 oz. Chocolate syrup
1 ½ oz vanilla syrup
4oz. Milk
3 cups crushed ice
Whipped cream
shaved chocolate

Blend all ingredients, except whipped cream and shaved chocolate until smooth. Garnish with whipped cream and shaved chocolate. Try white chocolate syrup with any fruit flavored syrup for a completely different result. Serves 2

Blueberry Ice Cream Soda

(Substitute your favorite syrup)

1 cup coffee flavored ice cream
double espresso, cooled
4 ounces blueberry flavored syrup
chilled club soda

Divide ice cream between 2 chilled stemmed glasses.
Pour flavored espresso over the ice cream. Now add the club soda to create the ice cream fizz. Stir and enjoy. Serves 2

Cinnanut Smoothie

6 scoops vanilla ice cream
3oz hazelnut syrup
3 oz cinnamon syrup
Two double espressos
Combine all in blender and blend until smooth
Serves 2

Vanilla Espresso Supreme

4 double espressos, cooled
2 cups milk
4 shots vanilla syrup
your favorite vanilla ice cream
whipped cream
Combine espresso, milk, and vanilla syrup

Stir together. Put a scoop of ice cream into each of 4 glasses. Pour espresso flavored milk over ice cream. Top with whipped cream. Vary with any ice cream and any syrup. Try lemon ice cream and mango syrup for a tropical smoothie. Serve with a straw and long handled spoon. Serves 4

Versatility! As you can see, there are many ways to get creative with espresso roast coffee. I created a quick and easy iced espresso frappuccino. I don't measure; all I do is pour as much hot chocolate cocoa powder into the bottom of my blender as I want, eyeball the ice up to about ½ full, add a long double espresso shot and blend. Simple, and super refreshing on hot afternoons. Try it. I know you'll like it.

Utilizing Coffee In Entrees

Coffee in the evening, coffee in the morning, coffee in the afternoon. ..
It had to happen. Somewhere, sometime, somebody decided it wasn't enough to just drink their brew; they had to cook with it. I thoroughly embrace the notion. I have other passions other than coffee. They involve eating and spices. Make me a curry that brings the sweat out on my forehead and I'll be your friend for life. Try my spicy rub for a nice change of pace.

My Spicy Rub

2 tablespoons ground coffee beans
2 tablespoons ground black pepper
1 ½ tablespoons kosher salt
½ teaspoon cayenne pepper
1 tablespoon curry powder

Preheat your oven's broiler. Place the ground coffee on a sheet of aluminum foil, and place on the top shelf. Broil for about 45 seconds, shaking the foil about every 10 seconds until it becomes slightly smoky.

In a small bowl, stir together the coffee, black pepper, salt, cayenne pepper, and curry powder. Rub into steaks. Let sit loosely covered in fridge 1 to 2 hours before cooking. I also do this with kebabs if I'm in the mood for grilled vegetables. Grill as desired. Serve with mango chutney.

People these days are in too much of a hurry. They want to keep up with the Joneses. Bigger homes. Better cars. It doesn't take much to make me happy. I live a simple life . . . Here are a few simple tips regarding cooking and coffee.

I found out long ago that coffee adds that certain something to any dish made with tomatoes. Add a new depth to a bowl of tomato soup by adding coffee. Enhance your favorite tomato sauce with coffee. It adds another dimension. Anybody you cook for will love your sauce and have no idea about your secret ingredient (unless you divulge it!). I believe that the acidity in the coffee and the acidity in the tomatoes join in unison. Experiment! Sliced tomatoes marinated in coffee for a few minutes then dipped in seasoned bread crumbs and baked? Hmmm...

Store bought marinades for meat are very popular. Here's a secret. Take your favorite marinade and push it up another notch by adding any dark roasted brew. Simple, but effective!

Speaking of marinades, here are a few that are quite good.

Coffee Marinade #1

1 cup dark roast coffee
¾ cup brown sugar
½ cup cider vinegar
½ cup finely minced onion
1 tablespoon olive oil
1 teaspoon dry mustard
1 ½ tsp ground black pepper

Combine all ingredients. Store covered in your refrigerator Marinate meat at least 2 hours (the longer the better) before grilling. This marinade goes great with beef or pork.

Coffee Marinade #2

½ cup vegetable oil
¼ cup lemon juice
¼ cup red wine vinegar
¼ cup dark roast coffee
1 teaspoon Dijon mustard
½ teaspoon curry powder
¼ teaspoon rosemary
¼ teaspoon thyme
¼ teaspoon savory
1 teaspoon salt
¼ teaspoon pepper

Combine all ingredients. Keep covered in your refrigerator- Marinate meat at least 2 hours (the longer the better) before grilling. This marinade goes great with lamb.

Marinades definitely don't need to be measured. Using coffee as your base and your imagination, create your own signature soak. Try different wines or spirits. Alternate vinegars and spices. Fresh vegetables come to mind, particularly onions, ginger, and garlic. (Garlic and ginger are vegetables, aren't they?) Honey, molasses, and brown sugar will caramelize, giving you a tasty glaze. Sauces such as soy or Worcestershire add taste and saltiness. Try varying your home-made marinade with different mustards.

Now yer cookin'…..

From marinades to sauces… here are a few back yard winners.

French Pressed BBQ Sauce

½ cup French pressed espresso coffee
1 cup ketchup
¼ cup red wine vinegar
¾ cup firmly packed dark brown sugar
1 cup onion--peeled and chopped
2 cloves garlic--peeled and crushed
2 tablespoons dark molasses
3 fresh hot chili peppers seeded and minced
2 tablespoons hot dry mustard mixed with 1
1 tablespoon water
2 tablespoons Worcestershire sauce
2 tablespoons ground cumin
2 tablespoons chili powder

Combine all ingredients in a saucepan and simmer over low heat for 20 minutes. Cool, then puree in a blender until smooth. Keep refrigerated.

French Roast BBQ Sauce

1 cup onion- chopped
2 tablespoons garlic - minced
1 tablespoon unsalted butter
¼ cup sherry vinegar
3 whole guerilla chilies -- stems removed and crushed
1 cup French roast coffee
1 ¼ cups tomato puree
⅓ cup molasses
½ teaspoon salt
½ teaspoon freshly ground black pepper

Sauté onion in butter over low-medium heat until soft. Add garlic and sauté for another two minutes. Deglaze the pan with sherry vinegar. Add all other ingredients and simmer over low heat until the chilies are very soft. Puree the sauce in a blender until very smooth. Strain through a sieve. Keep refrigerated.

An alternative to a marinade or BBQ sauce is of course a rub. Try these.

Coffee Rub # 1

4 tsp ground coffee
½ tsp garlic powder
¼ tsp paprika
⅛ tsp cayenne
1 tsp salt
½ tsp black pepper
½ tsp parsley flakes

Two rubs. Two totally different textures. Rub # 1 is great on beef; rub # 2 goes well with pork.

Coffee Rub # 2

¼ cup finely ground espresso beans
¼ cup firmly packed dark brown sugar
6 to 8 cloves garlic, chopped
2 to 3 teaspoons grated fresh ginger
3 to 4 teaspoons ground cardamom
Salt and pepper to taste

All rubbed meat should stand for one to two hours prior to grilling.

Coffee Peppered Steak

(Is it a rub? You decide.)

2 tablespoons whole bean coffee
2 tablespoons whole black peppercorns
2 one inch thick New York strip steaks
vegetable oil
kosher salt

Coarsely grind the coffee beans and peppercorns in a coffee grinder. Press the mixture evenly on both sides of the steaks. Let the steaks sit refrigerated, loosely covered in foil for a few hours. Lightly brush the grill with vegetable oil. Grill the steaks directly over high heat, turning once after 5 minutes. Cook another 3 to 5 minutes, and then remove the steaks from the grill. Season both sides with salt. Allow to rest for 2 - 3 minutes before serving. Serves 2

My favorite side for any barbecue dish.

Vidalia Onions with Espresso
(Substitute yellow onions)

4 Vidalia onions—sliced
4 tbsp butter
2 tsp sugar
3 double shots espresso
½ c chicken stock

Heat the butter in a skillet. Add the onions, season with salt and freshly ground pepper. Sauté until just softened. Add the sugar and cook another minute. Add the coffee and chicken stock. Continue to cook, stirring occasionally until the liquid reduces, approximately 15 to 20 minutes.

Oh, yeah--don't forget the vinaigrette!

Coffee Vinaigrette #1
This easy vinaigrette can be used for salads or as an accompaniment to grilled beef, shrimp, or pork.

1 ½ teaspoons coffee, very finely ground
½ teaspoon salt
1 teaspoon sugar
½ teaspoon freshly ground pepper
¼ cup sherry wine vinegar
½ cup extra virgin olive oil

Combine dry ingredients and vinegar. Slowly whisk in olive oil until well incorporated. Refrigerate until ready to serve. Makes 2-3 servings

Coffee Vinaigrette #2

1 tbsp dark brewed coffee
¼ cup balsamic vinegar
Salt & Pepper
¾ to 1 cup olive oil

Whisk all ingredients thoroughly. Add herbs and spices to suit your taste.

Heartier dishes which will satisfy everyone's appetite.

Beef Stew with Coffee

1 pound rump roast
¼ teaspoon salt
¼ teaspoon black pepper
1 ½ cups dark roast coffee
1 cup un-salted beef broth
½ cup finely chopped onion
½ cup dry red wine
2 garlic cloves -- minced
1 cup diced peeled potato
1 cup sliced mushrooms
1 tablespoon capers
1 cup diced tomatoes

Cut beef into 1-inch cubes. Sprinkle with salt and pepper. Put your saucepan over medium-high heat. Add beef, and cook until browned on all sides. Add coffee, broth, onion, wine and garlic, bring to just under a boil. Cover, reduce heat, and simmer 45 minutes. After 45 minutes, add tomatoes, mushrooms, potatoes, and capers; bring to a boil. Cover, reduce heat, and simmer another 20 minutes. Serve over rice. Serves 4

My Coffee Pot Roast

6 Carrots; peeled; cubed
2 cups potatoes; peeled; cubed
2 lb beef pot roast
Salt; pepper
1 cup canned tomatoes
1 cup dark roast black coffee
1 cup Water

Put vegetables in slow cooker. Salt and pepper the roast liberally. Place beef into cooker along with tomatoes, coffee, and water. Cover and cook on low heat 8 - 10 hours or until tender. Serves 4

My Favorite Cornish Hen Recipe

½ cup coffee flavored liqueur
¼ cup fresh orange juice
½ teaspoon fresh lemon juice
½ teaspoon prepared mustard
¼ teaspoon ground paprika
3 tablespoons unsalted butter
4 Cornish game hens
salt and pepper to taste
2 slices orange, halved
2 slices lemon, halved

Preheat oven to 375 degrees F. In a small saucepan, stir

together the coffee liqueur, orange and lemon juices, mustard and paprika. Add butter and bring to a boil. Once boiling, lower heat and simmer for 1 minute. Remove from heat, cover and set aside. Season the cavities of the hens with salt and pepper. Stuff each bird with half a slice of orange and half a slice of lemon. Spoon a tablespoon of the sauce into each hen. Truss the legs together with string and place breast side up in a shallow roasting pan, covering loosely with foil. Roast for 30 minutes in the preheated oven. Remove and discard foil. Baste hens with the coffee liqueur sauce. Continue roasting for an additional 30 minutes, basting a few more times, and reserving some of the sauce. Remove hens to a serving platter and remove strings. Place roasting pan onto the stovetop and deglaze with the remaining basting sauce. Simmer until thickened, then spoon over roasted hens. Garnish with remaining lemon and orange slices. Serves 4

Coffee Brisket

4 pounds brisket of beef
3 cloves garlic, slivered
3 cloves garlic, crushed
4 large onions, thinly sliced
1 cup apple cider vinegar
1-½ Tbsp bacon fat
1 cup dark roast coffee
salt and pepper, to taste
½ cup water

With a long thin, sharp knife make slits in the meat and insert the slivers of garlic. Place the meat in a bowl, spread 1 sliced onion and the crushed garlic over it, and pour in the vinegar. Marinate for 6 hours at room temperature or overnight in the refrigerator, turning several times. When ready to cook, preheat the oven to 350 degrees F. Heat the bacon fat in a deep, heavy skillet large enough to hold the brisket. Remove the brisket from the marinade and discard the onion and vinegar. Dry with paper towels. Brown the meat well on all sides. Remove brisket to a platter. In the fat remaining in the skillet, sauté the remaining sliced onions until deeply browned. Pour in ½ cup coffee. Bring to a boil, stirring and scraping the bottom of the skillet to loosen the browned bits. Spread the onions and liquid from the skillet in a shallow baking dish. Place the brisket on the onions. Season with salt and freshly ground pepper to taste. Pour in the remaining coffee and water. Cover tightly with foil and place in oven for ½ hour. Turn the oven down to 250 degrees F. and bake for an additional 2 hours or until meat is very tender. Slice the brisket thinly on an angle against the grain. Skim the fat from the pan liquid. Return the meat slices to the pan. Serves 6-8

Molasses-Coffee Glazed Ham

(A winner last Easter)

1 cup molasses
1 (12-ounce) jar apricot jam
2 tablespoons cider vinegar
1 tablespoon Dijon mustard
1 teaspoon salt
1 teaspoon vanilla extract
¾ cup brewed strong coffee
1 (8- to 9-pound) bone-in, fully cooked smoked ham half

Stir together all ingredients until blended. Reserve 1 cup of the molasses-coffee sauce in a small bowl and set aside.
Place ham in a lightly greased 13- x 9-inch pan. Pour remaining molasses-coffee sauce evenly over ham.
Bake, on lower rack, at 350° for 2 hours or until a meat thermometer registers 140°, basting with sauce in pan every 15 minutes. Cover loosely with lightly greased aluminum foil the last 30 minutes to prevent excessive browning, if necessary. Remove ham from baking pan; let rest at room temperature 30 minutes. Heat reserved molasses-coffee sauce, and serve with ham. Serves 8

O.K. Enough of the meat, let's try something sweet!

Utilizing Coffee In Desserts

In the early eighties, when I got out of high school, my parents owned a coffee shop in the city of Kitchener, Ontario, Canada. It was named Tea for Two Fine Coffees. Why Tea for Two when we sold coffee you might ask? I don't know. It just sounded catchy. We sold gourmet coffee by the cup along with many varieties of muffins, cookies and pastries; all made from scratch. Whole bean coffee and specialty coffee drink sales were secondary. We did, however, sell espresso coffee by the demitasse cup. I devised my favorite coffee based dessert in those early days and still enjoy it today. The combination, though incredibly simple, is incredibly good...a scoop of vanilla ice cream, topped with a double espresso and coconut flavored whipped cream...

My Coffee Mmmuffins

Stir to mix, and then sift together:
2 cups all purpose flour
2 tsp double acting baking powder
1 tsp baking soda
3 tbsp Turkish ground espresso roast coffee
½ tsp salt

In a separate bowl, lightly beat two eggs. Add to them:
½ cup sweet butter, melted and cooled
½ cup Bodum pressed espresso coffee, cooled
⅔ tsp vanilla extract
⅔ cup granulated white sugar.

Stir to mix. Add wet mixture to dry mixture and fold until moistened. Stir in ½ lb of chocolate chips Fill muffin cups ¾ full and bake 16 18 minutes at 350 degrees.

My Coffee Icing

In a small pan melt 4 tbsp sweet butter. Remove from heat and add ¼ cup Bodum pressed espresso coffee, cooled. Beat in confectioner's sugar until you reach a smooth, spread able consistency. Enjoy your muffins over bowlfuls of rich, black coffee. Black coffee enhances the sweetness of the muffin.

Tip: Buy an ice cream scoop to fill your muffin baking cups.

Before I share some awesome desserts, I have to give you a cure for any coffee lovers snack attack. These can also be used to garnish your favorite drink or dessert.

Coffee Roasted Almonds

1 c almonds
1 tbsp vegetable oil
1 c finely ground coffee
1 tsp garlic powder
1 tsp salt
1 tsp ground nutmeg
½ tsp cayenne pepper

Preheat oven to 350° F. Mix nuts and oil in a small bowl. Place nuts on baking sheet and bake for 8 to 10 minutes, or until lightly toasted. Pour dry ingredients into a slightly larger bowl, and then mix in nuts until well-coated. Return nuts to baking sheet and toast for 2 more minutes. Serve warm or at room temperature.

Chocolate Covered Espresso Beans

1 c espresso coffee beans
4 oz. milk chocolate
3 tablespoons of cocoa

Preheat oven to 350° F. Place coffee beans on baking pan

and roast for 8 to 10 minutes. (This will make beans lighter and crunchier) Remove from oven and let cool. In double boiler, melt chocolate until very creamy. Add coffee beans and stir until completely coated. Remove with slotted spoon allowing excess chocolate to drip off. Place beans on waxed paper so they do not stick together. Once the coffee beans have cooled sufficiently, but the chocolate is still a little soft, roll the beans in your hands to form round balls. Roll each one in cocoa and set aside until chocolate has hardened. Makes 1½ cups.

SWEEET…..

(Remember, all recipes can be made kid friendly by simply using decaf coffee)

Every recipe I have presented thus far contains coffee-- I'm going to stray here a little bit. There are certain cookies or pastries that just seem like the ideal fit to go with a hot cup of joe. The following are my two favorite little indulgences. The first is the perfect accompaniment to regular brewed coffee; the second complements the strength of espresso.

Biscotti

(the perfect partner to coffee)

Mention biscotti, and the first response will be "that's my favorite Italian cookie." In fact, the twice baked cookies can actually be traced back to the Romans. The name biscotti (biscotto) is derived from the Latin bis (twice) and cotto (cooked or baked). The Roman legion had soldiers afoot, trying to increase the empire. It was found that by partially baking, then cutting and re-baking the biscotti, they had a shelf life of nearly 6 months. Perfect for the long journeys the Roman soldiers faced. Throughout the centuries many races adapted the cookie and still have their own versions. The early explorers who set off for far and unknown lands even had their own version--the sea biscuit. I'm sure that many a sailor was as equally happy to see dry land as well as an end to the sea biscuit. Today, we view the cookie in a totally different light. Sometime, somewhere, somebody had a novel idea. The region of Tuscany, Italy produces excellent wines. Why not take a crisp, twice baked biscotti and dip it into a glass of local wine? The perfect dessert treat. We coffee lovers however have adapted our own twist. Gone is the graceful dip. We prefer the not so graceful dunk. Hey, it's a coffee thing. So dunk, coffee lovers, dunk!

5 eggs
1 ½ c. sugar
½ c. butter, melted
1 tsp. vanilla
½ tsp. anise extract

1 tsp. salt
¼ tsp. anise seeds(optional)
1 tsp. baking powder
4 ½ c. white flour
1 ½ c. walnuts, chopped
Butter for baking sheets

Preheat oven to 350 degrees. Beat eggs until fluffy; add sugar and melted butter. Mix well. Add vanilla, anise extract, and seeds; mix well. Add baking powder and flour in 3 additions, mixing well after each addition. Stir in walnuts. Lightly butter 1 large or 2 small cookie sheets. On a floured board, and using lightly floured hands shape the dough into 4 loaves 1 ½ inches in diameter and about 8 ½ inches long. Place loaves on cookie sheets 3 inches apart. Bake loaves for 25 minutes or until lightly browned. Take out loaves and turn oven down to 300 degrees. When loaves are cool enough to touch, cut diagonally into slices. Turn cookies onto their side and place back in oven for 5 minutes. Turn Biscotti over and toast 5 minutes more. Cool Biscotti and place in tin can with tight fitting lid. The cookies only taste better with age. You can keep biscotti for up to 6 months. If they lose their crunchiness, simply toast them in a 250 degree oven for a few minutes. Makes about 2 dozen biscotti.

Baklava

(the perfect partner to espresso)

Mention baklava, and the first response will be- "that's my favorite Greek pastry". In fact, the delicate thin pastry dough used to make baklava- 'phyllo'- does mean leaf in the Greek language. This refers to the leaf-like thinness of the dough which results in the airy layers of the finished pastry. However, the origins of baklava can be traced to 8th century Assyria. The Assyrians are believed to be the first to bake layered nuts, honey and dough together, using the ingredients plentiful in the region. Throughout the centuries the recipe spread and was embraced by many races in the Middle East--the Armenians, Turks, Lebanese, Persians, to name a few. Envision a sheik with his harem, indulging in a sweet honey dripping treat. The Greeks are credited for perfecting the heavier dough by introducing 'phyllo', thus in many minds, baklava is indeed Greek.

Syrup

1 cup sugar
1 cup honey
¾ cup water
1 tbsp lemon juice
2 cinnamon sticks
1" by 2" lemon peel
2 pinches ground clove
2 pinches ground cardamom
1 lb thawed phyllo dough, thawed in the refrigerator

Nut Mixture

¾ lb walnuts, chopped
¼ lb almonds, slivered
2 tsps ground cinnamon
¼ tsp salt
1 ½ cups unsalted butter

Combine the ingredients listed under syrup in a medium saucepan. Cook over medium heat, stirring occasionally, until the sugar is dissolved. Reduce the heat to medium-low and cook until the syrup is slightly thickened, about 10 minutes. Remove the cinnamon sticks and lemon peel and set aside to cool.

Preheat your oven to 350°.

Place nuts in food processor. Pulse a few times just to get a rough chop. Add the cinnamon and salt, and pulse briefly again to combine.

Melt the butter over low heat in a small saucepan.

Using a pastry brush, lightly coat a 9-by-13-inch baking dish with some of the melted butter.

Unfold the phyllo and cut to size of inside of baking dish. Cover phyllo with a slightly damp towel while you're working with it so that it doesn't dry out.

Place one of the sheets of phyllo in the bottom of the buttered baking dish and lightly brush with some of the melted butter. Repeat this procedure with 6 more sheets of phyllo, for a total of 7 layers. Sprinkle ¾ cup of the nut mixture evenly over the buttered phyllo sheets. Repeat again with 7 more sheets of phyllo, buttering each layer as before, and top these sheets with another ¾ cup of the nut mixture. Continue this layering process, buttering 7 sheets of phyllo and topping each 7 sheets with nuts, until you have used all of the nut mixture. Layer any remaining sheets of phyllo on top, buttering between each layer, until all of the phyllo sheets have been used.

Using a sharp steak knife, make four lengthwise cuts through the layered phyllo at 1½ -inch increments. You should have 5 strips lengthwise. Now cut diagonally at 1½ -inch increments to form diamond shapes. You should end up with approximately 36 diamond-shaped pieces of baklava. Bake the baklava until golden brown, about 40 minutes.

Remove from the oven, set aside on a wire rack to cool 5 minutes. Using a ladle, drizzle the cooled syrup over the warm baklava. Allow to stand at least several hours or overnight before serving. Your baklava can be stored at room temperature in an air tight container for up to two weeks.

Coffee Caramel Fondue

14 oz. caramels
¼ cup French roast coffee
¼ cup whole milk

Combine caramels, coffee and milk in a large microwaveable bowl. Microwave, stirring occasionally until caramels are completely melted and mixture is well blended. This wonderful dip can be served with assorted fresh fruits, cookies, or cake, anything sweet you can cut into pieces and dip. For a luxuriant twist, use chocolate caramels.

Chocolate Coffee Sauce

⅓ cup dark roast brewed coffee
½ cup firmly packed dark brown sugar
½ cup unsweetened cocoa powder
⅛ teaspoon salt
2 tablespoons unsalted butter, cut into pieces
½ teaspoon vanilla

In a saucepan over medium heat, whisk coffee with the brown sugar until the sugar is dissolved. Add the cocoa powder and the salt, and continue to whisk the mixture until it is smooth. Add the butter and the vanilla and whisk the sauce until the butter is melted. Serve the sauce warm over ice cream or cakes and pastries. Makes ¾ cups

Bananas in Coffee Cream Sauce

4 bananas, sliced
¼ c. coffee-flavored liqueur
½ c. whipping cream
1 tbsp. instant coffee (use for baking only! Drink only under extreme duress)
½ c. toasted almonds

Cut bananas into 1 inch thick round slices. Put into bowl, add coffee liqueur and toss gently to coat. Let marinate about 20 minutes. Arrange bananas in serving dish. Meanwhile beat cream until foamy. Add coffee crystals and beat just until soft peaks form. Spoon over bananas. Sprinkle with almonds. Serve immediately. Serves 4

Sauerkraut Cake

(An old German recipe; sounds strange, but it is really good)

2 ¼ cups all purpose flour
½ cup cocoa
1 tbsp baking powder
¼ tsp salt
1 tsp soda
⅔ cup butter
1 ½ cups sugar
3 large eggs
1 tsp vanilla
1 cup strong coffee
⅔ cup sauerkraut (drained and rinsed)

Combine first 5 ingredients. Cream butter and sugar; add eggs one egg at a time. Add vanilla to coffee. Beginning and ending with flour mixture, add liquid and dry ingredients alternately. Stir in sauerkraut and bake at 350 for 20-25 minutes in a 9X13 cake pan.

Quick 'n Easy Coffee Ice Cream Pie

18 Oreo cookies, crushed
⅛ stick butter, melted
1 qt. coffee ice cream
Pie tin

Combine crushed cookies and butter, press into a pie tin to create a shell. Soften ice cream just until spreadable. Spread into crust and freeze. Remove from freezer 10 to 15 minutes before serving. (I garnish this pie with mint flavored chocolate chips, and chocolate coffee sauce)

Coffee Almond Mousse

1 c brewed dark roast coffee
1 c non-fat dry milk powder
⅓ c sugar
1 tsp vanilla
1 envelope unflavored gelatin
¼ c cold water
½ c chopped almonds

Combine coffee and dry milk in mixer bowl. Put in freezer with beaters 30 minutes or until ice crystals form around edge. Remove and beat 10 minutes or until mixture forms peaks. Gradually beat in sugar; add vanilla and set aside. Sprinkle gelatin over water in small sauce pan. Cook and stir over low heat until gelatin dissolves. Gradually beat into whipped-milk mixture. Fold in nuts, and then pour into a large plastic container with an airtight lid. Freeze at least 6 hours. To serve scoop into ice cream cones, or simply enjoy out of a dessert cup. In an airtight container mousse will keep for a week. Makes about 1 ½ gallons

Coffee Granita Slush

4 cups strong brewed coffee
¾ cup sugar
2 tbsp honey
Pinch of cinnamon
Pinch of nutmeg

Add the sugar, honey, cinnamon, and nutmeg to a bowl. Slowly add the freshly brewed coffee and whisk well until the dry ingredients are dissolved. Pour the mixture into ice cube trays and freeze until hard. After the coffee cubes are frozen, put them in a food processor and blend until you have a coffee slush. Serve immediately in bowls topped with whipped cream. Serves 4

Chocolate Cake with Coffee

2 c sugar
¾ c. shortening
2 eggs
¾ c cocoa
2 c flour
1 tsp. baking powder
2 tsp baking soda
1 c dark roast coffee, cooled
1 c milk

Cream sugar and shortening. Add eggs and beat. Blend in cocoa. Sift 2 cups flour, baking powder and baking soda. Add alternately with coffee and milk. Bake at 375 degrees for 30 to 40 minutes

Coffee Kahlua Pie

1 (9 inch) baked pie shell
1 (5.33 oz.) can evaporated milk
½ c semi-sweet chocolate pieces
2 c miniature marshmallows
⅓ c toasted chopped almonds
⅓ c Kahlua liqueur
12 ounces whipped topping(go ahead- buy a tub at your grocery store)
Maraschino cherries
Combine evaporated milk and chocolate pieces in heavy

1 quart saucepan. Cook over low heat, stirring occasionally until chocolate melts completely and mixture thickens. Stir in marshmallows until melted. Remove from heat. Add almonds. Pour into a 2-quart bowl and refrigerate until cool (about 20 to 30 minutes), stirring twice. Add Kahlua, fold in whipped cream. Spoon into a baked pie shell. Freeze several hours until firm. Remove from freezer 10 minutes before serving. Garnish with additional whipped cream. Top with chopped almonds and cherries, if desired.

Mocha Rum Cake

3 cups all-purpose flour
1 ½ teaspoons baking soda
¾ teaspoon salt
¾ pound bittersweet chocolate, chopped
1 ½ cups unsalted butter, cut into pieces
⅓ cup dark rum
2 cups strong brewed coffee
2 ¼ cups granulated sugar
3 large eggs, beaten lightly
1 ½ teaspoons vanilla
confectioners' sugar for dusting
lightly sweetened whipped cream
cocoa powder for dusting

Preheat oven to 300°F. Butter a 12-cup bundt pan and dust with cocoa powder, knocking out excess. In a bowl whisk together flour, baking soda, and salt. In a large metal bowl set over a saucepan of barely simmering water melt chocolate and butter, stirring until smooth. Remove chocolate from heat and stir in rum, coffee, and granulated sugar. With an electric mixer beat in flour, ½ cup at a time. Scrape down sides and blend in. Beat in eggs and vanilla until batter is combined well. Pour batter into buttered and lightly floured pan. Bake cake in middle of oven until a tooth pick comes out clean, about 1 hour and 45 minutes. Let cake cool completely in pan on a rack and turn it out onto rack. Cake may be made 3 days in advance and kept wrapped well and chilled. Dust cake with confectioner's sugar to serve.

The only way I can end the recipe section of Celebrating the Bean is with a classic Italian recipe, Tiramisu. Oddly enough, as famous as it is, if you search Old Italian cookbooks you will find no word of it. The first mention ever comes from the early 1970's in Treviso, an Italian city northwest of Venice. It is said that the updated version of the base recipe was created in a restaurant in Treviso by the name of Le Beccherie. Although the traditional version has only been around since the early 1970's, Treviso is to this day famous world wide for its Tiramisu. Suffice it to say a journey into the origins and history of the now famous cake would be interesting, however for now I will simply give you my final recipe.

Classic Tiramisu

6 egg yolks
1 ¼ cups white sugar
1 ¼ cups mascarpone cheese
1 ¾ cups heavy whipping cream
2 (12 ounce) packages ladyfingers
¼ cup espresso roast coffee cooled, mixed with
¼ cup dark rum
1 teaspoon unsweetened cocoa powder, for dusting
2 or 3 squares of semisweet chocolate to garnish

Combine egg yolks and sugar in the top of a double boiler, over boiling water. Reduce heat to low, and cook for about 10 minutes, stirring constantly. Remove from heat and whip yolks and sugar until thick and lemon colored. Add mascarpone cheese to whipped yolks. Beat until combined. In a separate bowl, whip cream until it forms stiff peaks. Gently fold into yolk mixture and set aside. Split the lady fingers in half, and line the bottom and sides of a large glass bowl. Brush liberally with coffee/rum mixture. Spoon half of the cream filling over the lady fingers. Repeat ladyfingers, coffee/rum and filling layers. Garnish with cocoa powder and chocolate curls. Refrigerate several hours or overnight before serving. Tip…to make chocolate curls, use a vegetable peeler and run it down the edge of the chocolate squares.

Easy Tiramisu Ice Cream cake

(I can't resist a twist on the classic)

1 cup white sugar
⅔ cup water
1 ½ cups brewed espresso
⅓ cup coffee flavored liqueur
1 (9 inch) sponge cake
¼ cup finely ground espresso
2 pints espresso ice cream
2 pints coffee ice cream

Make a simple coffee syrup. In a small saucepan over medium heat, combine sugar and water. Bring to a boil, then remove from heat and stir in espresso and coffee liqueur. Let it cool completely. Split the sponge cake in half horizontally to make two layers. Place bottom layer in a serving dish. Brush with ½ of the coffee syrup. Sprinkle half of the ground espresso evenly over the surface of the cake. Beat the espresso ice cream with the paddle attachment of an electric mixer until spreadable. Spread over bottom cake layer. Place the top cake layer over the ice cream. Brush with remaining coffee syrup. Place in freezer for 30 minutes. Remove from freezer. Beat the coffee ice cream until spreadable. Spread the ice cream over the frozen cake, and swirl to make pretty. Sprinkle remaining ground espresso on top and return cake to freezer until firm.

Did You Know?

- My personal motto when writing Celebrating the Bean was to "pour myself into every page." I gave up my own personal will and let my thoughts flow because "God pushes the pen."

- The secretary of the Navy in 1913 was a man named Josephus Daniels, a teetotaler. He abolished alcohol on all naval ships, and from that time on the strongest beverage allowed was coffee--soon to be known as a cup of Joe.

- During the American Civil War, soldiers were issued eight pounds of coffee per every 100 pounds of food.

- The Egyptians are perceived to be coffee purists, preferring their brew black. Coffee is, however, served sweetened at weddings.

- Johann Sebastian Bach wrote a cantata to coffee in 1732.

- Over 25 million people are employed in the coffee industry.

- Many Japanese people believe that bathing in coffee grounds fermented with pineapple pulp softens the skin to prevent aging.

- The term espresso, although debated heatedly, is likely from the Latin word expresere, meaning 'to press out.'

- The country of Italy, as small as it is, has over 200,000 coffee bars.

- A burlap bag of imported coffee weighs approximately 130 pounds and contains roughly 600,000 coffee beans.

- I thoroughly enjoyed writing 'Celebrating the Bean.' I hope that you, fellow coffee fans, embrace the bean daily, as I do. Raise a mug of your favorite brew, as we

CELEBRATE THE BEAN!